Democratic Frontiers

Democratic Frontiers: Algorithms and Society focuses on digital platforms' effects in societies with respect to key areas such as subjectivity and self-reflection, data and measurement for the common good, public health and accessible datasets, activism in social media and the import/export of AI technologies relative to regime type.

Digital technologies develop at a much faster pace relative to our systems of governance which are supposed to embody democratic principles that are comparatively timeless, whether rooted in ancient Greek or Enlightenment ideas of freedom, autonomy and citizenship. Algorithms, computing millions of calculations per second, do not pause to reflect on their operations. Developments in the accumulation of vast private datasets that are used to train automated machine learning algorithms pose new challenges for upholding these values. Social media platforms, while the key driver of today's information disorder, also afford new opportunities for organized social activism. The US and China, presumably at opposite ends of an ideological spectrum, are the main exporters of AI technology to both free and totalitarian societies. These are some of the important topics covered by this volume that examines the democratic stakes for societies with the rapid expansion of these technologies.

Scholars and students from many backgrounds as well as policy makers, journalists and the general reading public will find a multidisciplinary approach to issues of democratic values and governance encompassing research from Sociology, Digital Humanities, New Media, Psychology, Communication, International Relations and Economics.

Michael Filimowicz is Senior Lecturer in the School of Interactive Arts and Technology (SIAT) at Simon Fraser University. He has a background in computer-mediated communications, audiovisual production, new media art and creative writing. His research develops new multimodal display technologies and forms, exploring novel form factors across different application contexts including gaming, immersive exhibitions and simulations.

Algorithms and Society

Series Editor:
Dr Michael Filimowicz *is Senior Lecturer in the School of Interactive
Arts and Technology (SIAT) at Simon Fraser University.*

As algorithms and data flows increasingly penetrate every aspect of our lives, it is imperative to develop sufficient theoretical lenses and design approaches to humanize our informatic devices and environments. At stake are the human dimensions of society which stand to lose ground to calculative efficiencies and performance, whether at the service of government, capital, criminal networks, or even a general mob concatenated in social media.

Algorithms and Society is a new series which takes a broad view of the information age. Each volume focuses on an important thematic area, from new fields such as software studies and critical code studies to more established areas of inquiry such as philosophy of technology and science and technology studies. This series aims to stay abreast of new areas of controversy and social issues as they emerge with the development of new technologies.

If you wish to submit a book proposal for the series, please contact Dr Michael Filimowicz michael_f@sfu.ca or Emily Briggs emily.briggs@tandf.co.uk

Digital Totalitarianism
Algorithms and Society
Edited by Michael Filimowicz

Privacy
Algorithms and Society
Edited by Michael Filimowicz

Systemic Bias
Algorithms and Society
Edited by Michael Filimowicz

Democratic Frontiers
Algorithms and Society
Edited by Michael Filimowicz

Deep Fakes
Algorithms and Society
Edited by Michael Filimowicz

For more information on the series, visit: https://www.routledge.com/Algorithms-and-Society/book-series/ALGRAS

Democratic Frontiers
Algorithms and Society

**Edited by
Michael Filimowicz**

Routledge
Taylor & Francis Group

LONDON AND NEW YORK

First published 2022
by Routledge
4 Park Square, Milton Park, Abingdon, Oxon OX14 4RN

and by Routledge
605 Third Avenue, New York, NY 10158

Routledge is an imprint of the Taylor & Francis Group, an informa business

British Library Cataloguing-in-Publication Data
A catalogue record for this book is available from the British Library

Library of Congress Cataloging-in-Publication Data
Names: Filimowicz, Michael, editor.
Title: Democratic frontiers : algorithms and society / edited by Michael Filimowicz.
Description: First Edition. | New York, NY : Routledge, 2022. |
Series: Algorithms and society | Includes bibliographical references and index.
Identifiers: LCCN 2021053487 (print) | LCCN 2021053488 (ebook) |
ISBN 9781032002675 (hardback) | ISBN 9781032002712 (paperback) |
ISBN 9781003173427 (ebook)
Subjects: LCSH: Algorithms—Social aspects. | Internet—Social aspects. | Databases—Social aspects. | Democracy.
Classification: LCC HM851 .D456 2022 (print) | LCC HM851 (ebook) |
DDC 302.23/1—dc23/eng/20220104
LC record available at https://lccn.loc.gov/2021053487
LC ebook record available at https://lccn.loc.gov/2021053488

ISBN: 978-1-032-00267-5 (hbk)
ISBN: 978-1-032-00271-2 (pbk)
ISBN: 978-1-003-17342-7 (ebk)

DOI: 10.4324/9781003173427

Typeset in Times New Roman
by codeMantra

The Open Access version of chapter 2 was funded by The Weizenbaum Institute

The Open Access version of chapter 3 was funded by Wellcome Trust, via King's College London, UK

Contents

Illustrations

Figures

Table

Contributors

Dr Mercedes Bunz is Reader in Digital Society and Deputy Head of the Department of Digital Humanities, King's College London. Her research explores how machine learning transforms knowledge and with it power, in particular in the medical sector, where she leads a research project supported by the Wellcome Trust. Her last publication is *The Internet of Things* with Graham Meikle and 'The calculation of meaning: on the misunderstanding of new artificial intelligence as culture' published in the journal *Culture, Theory and Critique.*

Kristin Comeforo (PhD, Rutgers University) is an associate professor of Communication at the University of Hartford, teaching specifically in the area of Advertising. Committed to feminist methods and pedagogies, Kristin applies an intersectional feminist perspective to inform the struggle against capitalism, the patriarchy and other systems of oppression. Their eclectic research agenda includes work related to how feminism, social justice, gender, LGBTQ+ identities and lived experience are mediated through digital and social media.

Rainer Diaz-Bone is a professor of sociology, with a focus on qualitative and quantitative methods at the University of Lucerne, Switzerland. With a background in social sciences and applied social research, his dissertation was awarded the Dissertation prize by the German Sociological Association. His main areas of research are methodical and theoretical foundations of social sciences, economic and cultural sociology and French neopragmatic and neostructuralist sociology.

Arhan Sabri Ertan is an assistant professor of International Trade at Boğaziçi University. Previously, he served as a visiting assistant professor of economics at Brown, New York, Boston, Northeastern and Tufts universities. His research interest spans various topics related to economic development (with a long-term and institutional perspective), behavioral economics (focusing on the role of personal characteristics and the efficiency of institutions), international economics (both trade and finance) and international conflict. In his research, which is mostly empirical and interdisciplinary, he is aiming to provide new perspectives for explaining the developmental differences and problems observed around the globe. Dr. Ertan holds a PhD in Economics from Brown University.

Eran Fisher is an associate professor at the Department of Sociology, Political Science and Communication, the Open University of Israel. He studies technology and society, with a special interest in digital media, digital work and capitalism, big data and algorithms, and media history. His books include *Media and New Capitalism in the Digital Age* (Palgrave, 2010), *Internet and Emotions* (Routledge, 2014; co-edited with Tova Benski), *Reconsidering Value and Labour in the Digital Age* (Palgrave, 2015; co-edited with Christian Fuchs) and *Algorithms and Subjectivity: The Subversion of Critical Knowledge*, which is forthcoming with Routledge.

Berna Görgülü holds a Masters degree in Communication from the University of Hartford. With a critical perspective on capitalism and all the social privileges it brings, Berna's research interests include feminism, digital media, capitalism, and the transformative relationship between them. She has deep experience as a feminist in Turkey, where she played a pivotal role in writing and winning parliamentary approval for law no. 6284, which is the only legal protection of women against violence in Turkey. She is an active member of the #IstanbulConventionSavesLives movement, as well as being the founding member and first president of the We Will Stop Femicide Platform.

Simon Schrör is a sociologist and research group lead at Weizenbaum Institute for the Networked Society and the Humboldt University of Berlin. He holds a degree in sociology and an MA with distinction in sociology, with a focus on transnationalization and society comparison from University Duisburg-Essen. His works focus on the normative foundations of digitization, intellectual property and cultural economy with a PhD Project covering the digital implications on the design furniture industry. His interdisciplinary research group "Shifts in Norm Setting" consists of legal and sociology scholars.

Hamid Akın Ünver is an associate professor of International Relations at Özyeğin University and a nonresident fellow of Carnegie Endowment's Digital Democracy Network. Previously, he served as a research fellow at the Oxford Internet Institute, Oxford Artificial Intelligence Society and the Alan Turing Institute in London. His research interests include technology and politics, computational social science and conflict research. Akin holds a PhD in Government from the University of Essex and previously taught courses on social conflict at Princeton, Michigan, Essex and LSE. Dr. Unver is a member of the National Academy of Sciences of Turkey.

Dr Photini Vrikki is a Lecturer in Digital Media and Culture at the Department of Digital Humanities, King's College London. Her research and teaching focuses on links between social and digital inequalities; power and data; and algorithmic cultural developments. She has been awarded the Charlemagne Prize Fellowship 2020–2021 for her project "Toward Solidary European Data Spaces" where she explores the deployment of solidarity governance mechanisms and the role of data literacy in the European data economy.

Series Preface: Algorithms and Society

Michael Filimowicz

This series is less about what algorithms are and more about how they act in the world through "eventful" (Bucher, 2018, p. 48) forms of "automated decision making" (Noble, 2018, loc. 141) in which computational models are "based on choices made by fallible human beings" (O'Neil, 2016, loc. 126).

> Decisions that used to be based on human reflection are now made automatically. Software encodes thousands of rules and instructions computed in a fraction of a second.
>
> (Pasquale, 2015, loc. 189)

> If, in the industrial era, the promise of automation was to displace manual labor, in the information age it is to pre-empt agency, spontaneity, and risk: to map out possible futures before they happen so objectionable ones can be foreclosed and desirable ones selected.
>
> (Andrejevic, 2020, p. 8)

> [M]achine learning algorithms that anticipate our future propensities are seriously threatening the chances that we have to make possible alternative political futures.
>
> (Amoore, 2020, p. xi)

Algorithms, definable pragmatically as "a method for solving a problem" (Finn, 2017, loc. 408), "leap from one field to the next" (O'Neil, 2016, loc. 525). They are *hyperobjects*: things with such broad temporal and spatial reach that they exceed the phenomenological horizon of human subjects" (Hong, 2020, p. 30). While in the main the technological systems taken up as volume topics are design solutions to problems for which there are commercial markets, organized communities or claims of state interest, their power and ubiquity generate new problems for inquiry. The series will do its part to track this domain fluidity across its volumes and contest, through critique and investigation, their "logic of secrecy" (Pasquale, 2015, loc. 68) and "obfuscation" (loc. 144).

These new *social* (rather than strictly computational) problems that are generated can, in turn, be taken up by many critical, policy and speculative discourses. At their most productive, such debates can potentially alter the ethical, legal and even imaginative parameters of the environments in which the algorithms of our information architectures and infrastructures operate, as algorithmic implementations often reflect a "desire for epistemic purity, of knowledge stripped of uncertainty and human guesswork" (Hong, 2020, p. 20). The series aims to foster a general intervention in the conversation around these often "black boxed" technologies and track their pervasive effects in society.

> Contemporary algorithms are not so much transgressing settled societal norms as establishing new patterns of good and bad, new thresholds of normality and abnormality, against which actions are calibrated.
>
> (Amoore, 2020, p. 5)

Less "hot button" algorithmic topics are also of interest to the series, such as their use in the civil sphere by citizen scientists, activists and hobbyists, where there is usually not as much discursive attention. Beyond private, state and civil interests, the increasingly sophisticated technology-based activities of criminals, whether amateur or highly organized, deserve broader attention as now everyone must defend their digital identities. The information systems of companies and states conduct a general form of "ambient surveillance" (Pasquale, 2015, loc. 310), and anyone can be a target of a hacking operation.

Algorithms and Society thus aims to be an interdisciplinary series which is open to researchers from a broad range of academic backgrounds. While each volume has its defined scope, chapter contributions may come from many areas such as sociology, communications, critical legal studies, criminology, digital humanities, economics, computer science, geography, computational media and design, philosophy of technology and anthropology, along with others. Algorithms are "shaping the conditions of everyday life" (Bucher, 2018, p. 158) and operate "at the intersection of computational space, cultural systems, and human cognition" (Finn, 2017, loc. 160), so the multidisciplinary terrain is vast indeed.

Since the series is based on the shorter Routledge Focus format, it can be nimble and responsive to emerging areas of debate in fast-changing technological domains and their sociocultural impacts.

References

Amoore, L. (2020). *Cloud Ethics: Algorithms and the Attributes of Ourselves and Others*. Duke University Press.

Andrejevic, M. (2020). *Automated Media*. Taylor and Francis.

Bucher, T. (2018). *If...Then: Algorithmic Power and Politics*. Oxford University Press.

Finn, E. (2017). *What Algorithms Want: Imagination in the Age of Computing*. MIT Press. Kindle version.

Hong, S. H. (2020). *Technologies of Speculation: The Limits of Knowledge in a Data-Driven Society*. New York University Press.

Noble, S. U. (2018). *Algorithms of Oppression*. New York University Press. Kindle version.

O'Neil, C. (2016). *Weapons of Math Destruction*. Broadway Books. Kindle version.

Pasquale, F. (2015). *The Black Box Society*. Harvard University Press. Kindle version.

Volume Introduction

Michael Filimowicz
Democratic Frontiers takes up considerations of digital platforms' effects in societies with respect to key areas such as subjectivity and self-reflection, data and measurement for the common good, public health and accessible datasets, activism in social media and the import/export of AI technologies relative to regime type.

Chapter 1 – "Algorithmic Knowledge and the Subversion of Subjectivity" by Eran Fisher – analyzes digital platforms as epistemic media that go beyond communicating knowledge to generating it. Drawing on Habermas's conceptions of critical knowledge and self-reflection, these platforms are criticized for undermining human subjectivity by excluding self-reflection.

Chapter 2 – "Algorithms, Conventions and New Regulation Processes" by Rainer Diaz-Bone and Simon Schrör – discusses the French approach of economics and sociology of conventions which is designed to foster the common good through a focus on data quality and measurement frameworks. The opaque and privately held character of big data and its algorithms post new regulatory challenges for governance.

Chapter 3 – "From Big to Democratic Data: Why the Rise of AI Needs Data Solidarity" by Mercedes Bunz and Photini Vrikki – presents a case study on the role of public datasets to counter typical shortcomings in private data that are used to train machine learning algorithms and which too often rely on invisible data processes. They argue for the concept of "data solidarity" as a governance principle that favors democratic rather than economic factors in data practices.

Chapter 4 – "Democratic Possibilities of Digital Feminism: The Case of #IstanbulConventionSaves Lives and #IstanbulSozlesmesi" by Kristin Comeforo and Berna Görgülü – discusses the role of social media platforms and hashtag-defined social movements in Turkey to organize activism around the issue of femicide. Through close reading of over 25,000 tweets and interviews with women, the chapter identifies structural components of digital feminism.

Chapter 5 – "Politics of Artificial Intelligence Adoption: Unpacking the Regime Type Debate" by H. Akın Ünver and Arhan S. Ertan – examines the patterns and determinant factors of whether countries tend to import AI technology from the US or China. They find that while both countries export to authoritarian and democratic countries, the US supplies more technologies for policing and surveillance, debunking several myths associated with AI and regime preferences.

Acknowledgment

The chapter summaries here have in places drawn from the authors' chapter abstracts, the full versions of which can be found in Routledge's online reference for the volume.

1 Algorithmic Knowledge and the Subversion of Subjectivity

*Eran Fisher**

Introduction

One good reason to think about digital platforms as socially transformative is their ability, indeed propensity, to create new knowledge. The knowledge that they create – algorithmically rendered from
users' data – is not merely a commodity, sold to third-party actors
(Andrejevic, 2012; Fisher, 2015; Scholz, 2013; Zuboff, 2020); more
importantly, this knowledge makes part and parcel of digital media,
underlying and enabling its function. As knowledge becomes not just
the end-product of a system but also its condition of possibility, the
very nature and function of knowledge in society also changes. What
changes is *how* we know and what it *means* to know. Digital platforms,
dedicated to anything from retailing and streaming to dating and
navigating, are now acting primarily as major epistemic sites, devices
for the production and collection of data, and their processing into
knowledge. This technological drive toward *Knowing Machines* (Mac-
Kenzie, 1996) and *Knowing Capitalism* (Thrift, 2005) has been primarily propelled by personalization. This is, arguably, the epistemic
essence of digital media, what makes such media new: their ability
to create personal knowledge about their audience and provide them
with targeted information, be it movie recommendations on Netflix,
navigational instructions on Waze, or advertisements.

The generalized, homogenous audience of mass media has become
the personalized users of digital media. As individuals use platforms
(leaving a plethora of data traces), they also become known to them.
But a less straightforward process also takes place: as this knowledge
about users is reflected back at them – through visual and textual

* An earlier version of this article appeared as Fisher E. Epistemic media and critical
knowledge about the self: Thinking about algorithms with Habermas. Critical Sociology. September 2021. doi:10.1177/08969205211044193. Reprinted with permission.

means or simply through personalized content – it also informs their knowledge about themselves. An ever more intimate relationship is knitted with epistemic threads between humans and machines, as users' knowledge about the world and about their own self is mediated by digital platforms in real time and performatively (Afriat, Dvir-Gvirsman, Tsuriel, & Ivan, 2020; Bucher, 2012).

A cybernetic feedback loop between a knowing machine and a knowing human being, mediated by personal data and creating personalized knowledge, is a striking epistemic novelty: it changes how we know ourselves and what knowing oneself entails. Digital platforms can, therefore, be understood as knowledge devices or *epistemic media*, which translate users' data-producing behavior into an image of their self, of who they are in terms of personality, interests, habits, tastes, worldviews, and so forth.

To grasp the significance of digital media as epistemic devices – devices conducive to the production of knowledge – this chapter offers an analysis based on a historical-comparative approach to media. Such approach allows highlighting both the continuities in media as epistemic devices and the radical transformation which digital media bring about. To compare old and new media, and indeed diverse media forms and practices, I suggest the notion of epistemic media as a shared analytical coordinate. This notion highlights the epistemic functions (whether implicit or explicit) of media, which act not only to communicate existing information over space and time but which facilitate the creation of *new* knowledge. This new knowledge emerges from a triad consisting of media forms, media practices, and human agents. And it is this particular triad which gave us historically new ways to know the self through critical distance and self-reflection, the result of which was subjectivity.

Such a feat was not technologically determined but presupposed particular historical contingencies. The history of media is dotted with specific contingencies of media forms and practices that facilitated the emergence of modern subjectivity as a historically specific way of knowing oneself. Digital media are the latest reiteration of such epistemic media history. But as much as they continue this history and its relations to self-knowledge, they also constitute a radical break in this history, consequential for the relations between media and subjectivity in contemporary culture. Whereas old epistemic media facilitated the formation of subjectivity through the creation of reflective knowledge about the self (i.e., knowledge of the self about the self), digital media attempts to do away with self-reflection and present to the self nonreflective knowledge about itself. This undermines the formation of subjectivity. Elucidating the shift from (old) epistemic media as allowing a space for expanding the scope of subjectivity to (digital) epistemic media as contracting this scope is the purpose of this chapter.

I proceed by first suggesting to think about media as epistemic devices, which have been central to the construction of subjectivity in the West (I). I then present current research on what I call algorithmic knowledge in diverse media environments, highlighting why algorithmic devices should be thought of as epistemic media (II). Next, with the help of Jürgen Habermas's theory of knowledge (Habermas, 1972), I argue that the type of knowledge that algorithms create is different from previous epistemic media and is less likely to support a process of subjectivity formation (III). I conclude with the argument that as epistemic media, digital platforms work toward turning subjective and intersubjective knowledge into an objective one. They exclude reflection from the process of self-knowing, leading to knowledge about the self which is uncritical, and undermines the project of subjectivization (IV).

Media as Epistemic Devices

As people who write for a living, academics know well that writing is not merely about putting thoughts to paper (or to a computer screen), but rather a constructive process which involves mind and matter and which helps us form our arguments. Writing is a workshop where reasoning takes shape. In formal terms, we might say that writing is a networked process, a dispositif (Kessler, Chateau, & Moure, 2018). The resulting text is not merely a projection of preexisting knowledge, residing in the mind, but involves devices such as paper, pen, alphabet, formats, keyboards, and excerpts. This context of form and matter facilitates the weaving of certain forms of thought and expression. This idea is echoed in myth as well as in science. Nietzsche suggested that "our writing tools are also working on our thoughts" (cited in Kittler, 1999), and Kittler suggests that this was indeed the case with Nietzsche's writing when he took on a typewriter: "[Nietzsche's prose] changed from arguments to aphorisms, from thoughts to puns, from rhetoric to telegram style" (Kittler, 1999). Not only poetic interpretations, but experimental studies as well consider this effect, for example, studies showing how the keyboard's QWERTY layout affects the meaning of words. Users associate positive and negative connotations with the right- and left-hand sides of the keyboard. This has effects on language use, such as the choice of words (containing more "positive" or "negative" letters) and even baby names (Casasanto et al., 2014; Garcia & Strohmaier, 2016; Jasmin & Casasanto, 2012).

The most audacious attempt to theorize the complex interactions of people's bodies and minds with material and cultural artifacts within media studies has been made by the Toronto school, spanning from Harold Innis, through Walter Ong, to Marshall McLuhan. They all insisted on media – its materiality, form, and mode of operation – as a key independent variable exerting effects on other variables and hence worthy of its own analysis. They analyzed media as key in the formation of political power (Innis, 1995), political culture (Postman, 2005), ideology (Postman, 1993), cognitive-linguistic structures (Havelock, 1988; Ong, 1982), cultural forms (McLuhan, 2011), and even corporal, perceptual, and sensorial coordinates of human life (McLuhan, 1994).

Most pertinent to our investigation of media and knowledge is Friedrich Kittler, to a large extent an heir to that school, who thought of media in terms of "cultural techniques" (Young, 2015). Media are not merely *tabula rasa* on which meaning and knowledge are conveyed. Their very essence primes what meanings could be conveyed and what could be constituted as knowledge. Kittler turns our gaze to the epistemic character of media forms by revisiting Michel Foucault's notion of discourse. Whereas Foucault examines discourse by looking at the vocabulary and syntax of true statements and true practices, Kittler seeks to examine the media by which such vocabulary and syntax can even come to exist. Whereas Foucault and other post-structuralists look at language games, Kittler turns his gaze to the playing ground where such games take place. He seeks to lay bare the *media conditions* under which a given discursive universe can be formed. To reframe my research question in terms of Kittler's formulation, we might ask: what are the media conditions under which subjectivity can come to be? Kittler, then, suggests that the knowledge generated by epistemic media is also partially structured by them; it is knowledge that does not precede the media which allows it to be constructed and performed.

We can therefore think of epistemic media as generative and performative. They do not merely register and record but also order "fundamental terms and units ... organize and orient ... arrange people and property, often into a grid" (Peters, 2015, p. 37). Their epistemic function is not only exogenous, as a kin term – logistical media – may suggest. They organize and put into a grid not only "reality" or "the world" (Rossiter, 2016), but also the knowledge of ordering itself (Kittler, 1992). For example, a two-by-two table *a priori* suggests correlations (if not causality) between variables. As epistemic media organize the world on which they report, they also give rise to a meta-ordering concerning how to organize knowledge. Ordering knowledge, then, is itself a form of knowledge. We should therefore ask how epistemic media order knowledge and with what consequences. To the extent that these media create knowledge about the self, we should also unveil how they order that knowledge and with what consequences to the self.

Epistemic media take part in the construction of what Karin Knorr Cetina calls *Epistemic Cultures* (Knorr Cetina, 1999). Her empirical focus is directed at the epicenter of scientific knowledge, but it can very well be borrowed in order to think about self-knowledge emanating from digital media. Knorr Cetina turns her gaze from the construction of knowledge to "the construction of the machineries of knowledge construction" (Knorr Cetina, 1999, p. 3). Knorr Cetina refers to "machineries" or "devices" of knowledge primarily as a metaphor, and investigates how these are applied in real laboratories in the natural and exact sciences in order to create knowledge. We might turn the tables and think about the actual machineries of knowledge – media – while investigating them metaphorically as laboratories. We can therefore think of epistemic media as laboratories where knowledge is created and ask about the particular conditions under which they are created, how these devices of knowledge work, and the procedures and steps by which media forms, media practices, and media users create new knowledge about the self.

The generative nature of epistemic media has been explored in seminal works in the social sciences. Underlying many of these media is the explosion in information and the rationalization of knowledge production which has emerged with modern science (Blair, 2011; Burke, 2000; Hankins, 1985). Goody (1977, 1986) shows how lists acted as knowledge devices by decontextualizing and reorganizing information according to new epistemic categories such as importance or utility (see also Müller-Wille & Charmantier 2012). Krajewski (2011) points out the centrality of notes and index cards in the work of scientists since the 16th century, seeing them as "paper machines" involved in the construction of scientific knowledge. Heesen (2000) shows the impact that boxes and notes of 18th-century explorers had on the establishment of standard classification and taxonomy in natural history. The page (Mak, 2012), word processing (Kirschenbaum, 2016), the book (Houston, 2016), and the scroll (Kelly, 2019) have all been explored as theaters of communication which structure the message inscribed on them (McLuhan, 1994).

But how do epistemic media create knowledge? At the heart of that process is the ordering of data, as a raw material, in a particular way. Epistemic devices do not dictate *what* to think but *how* to think it; they facilitate a particular way of knowing reality by the force of their form and how they are being used. Epistemic media are characterized by the primacy of form over content. They are usually ultra-lean in terms of content and allow users to fill in the blanks (comprised of lines, rubrics, tables, spaces, etc.). Being fillable (Gitelman, 2014), they are also (relatively) open-ended, open for interpretation and customization by users. Last, epistemic media are primarily practical; they are *used* rather than merely read. The media practices involved in using them are likewise varied: a personal diary may be filled each night before bedtime (or early in the morning), it could be reread by its owner frequently (or on special occasions), it could be recited aloud to an intimate friend (or kept forever a secret), and so forth.

Epistemic Media and Subjectivity

The seminal works I mention underlie the performativity of epistemic media – the extent to which media take part in the construction of knowledge they are assumed merely to record. But there is a stronger claim that lurks in these works, which points to a link between epistemic media and subjectivity, a link which is neither determinist nor necessary, but contingent. Gitelman points as much in her study of a growing market of mass-produced media, beginning in the 19th century, designed for "incremental filling in, filling up" (Gitelman, 2014, p. 21): documents (see also Clanchy, 2013; Kafka, 2012; Vismann, 2008). She underscores the dual epistemic value of fillable media directed at the world and at the self: "Filling up evidently helped people locate goods, map transactions, and transfer value, *while it also helped them to locate themselves* or others within or against the sites, practices, and institutions that helped to structure daily life" (Gitelman, 2014, pp. 21–22, emphasis added). Although fillable media were sparely printed – lines, rubrics, dates – or precisely because of that, they "worked to structure knowledge and insatiate culture ..." (Gitelman, 2014, p. 24). But something even more radical happens with epistemic media. As they construct a particular view of the world, "revealing" its character, they also incidentally reveal a particular character of the revealer. In the case of documents, they constructed a particular type of "bureaucratic self" in the US during the second half of the 19th century (Gitelman, 2014, pp. 30–31).

The dual epistemic propensity of media – to structure knowledge about the world as well as about the user of media – is noted in two seminal works of social theory: Weber's and Habermas's. Weber points to the centrality of double-entry bookkeeping (or ledger) for the emergence of a particular sensibility of a self, prone to the rationalization of economic activity, and of life in general. Such an economizing, rationalizing self is central to the emergence of capitalism, but obviously has broader social ramifications (Weber, 1958). Weber shifts our attention from structural conditions priming the emergence of capitalism toward the interpretive world of actors who must partake in this new social formation. Central to this new worldview (or ethics), which allowed capitalism to come about and thrive, is the rationalization of social spheres which have hitherto not been subjected to this process, primarily the economy. Theological reasons aside, proto-capitalist Calvinist and Puritan business owners began conducting their business in a more rational manner, according to principles of calculation and prediction. One of the means to rationalize business conduct was record-keeping, and it is at that period, when capitalism started to gain traction, that double-entry bookkeeping came into dominance.

Up until the invention of the accounting ledger, business transactions, such as sales, expenses, loans, and debts, were recorded on "mere scraps of paper" or as entries in diaries "where the settlement of debts was indicated by the *effective though untidy method* of deletion" (Basil, 1947, p. 264, emphasis added). The essence of the new method was organizing and processing economic data in a "systematized" manner (Basil, 1947, p. 264). Bookkeeping was a novel means (involving a new media form and a new practice) to record business transactions, which allowed owners to create a new type of knowledge about their business by *objectifying* transactions and *monitoring* them over time. The ordering of data, registered in real time, and accumulated chronologically laid bare a new type of knowledge which had hitherto remained inaccessible. It allowed the media user to get a glimpse into the well-being of the business, to valuate previous investments (indeed, to render loans as financial investments), and to make better judgment concerning future ones.

The ledger then suggested to users that their knowledge of reality – including their knowledge of their own self – was limited and partial. Another epistemic media which provided the means to overcome this limitation and facilitated self-reflection was the personal diary (as well as personal letters), underscored in the work of Habermas on the public sphere. Habermas considers them as media forms that allowed authors to present themselves to themselves, thereby gaining a new sense of self-reflection and critical knowledge about the self: "Through letter writing the individual unfolded himself in his subjectivity" (Habermas, 1991, p. 48). Diary writing was not merely an "imprint of the soul" and a "visit of the soul" but also a way to make the self visible or public: "the diary became a letter addressed to the sender, and the first-person narrative became a conversation with one's self addressed to another person" (Habermas, 1991, p. 49). The consequence of this engagement with media, Habermas dubbed "experiments with … subjectivity", centered on "audience-oriented privacy" (Habermas, 1991, p. 51). It was as if a mirror was put inside the private sphere of the self, adding a new gaze and a new dimension, through which to experience the self.

The diary was a radically new invention linking self to knowledge through media. As Habermas puts it, the 18th century "reveled and felt at ease in a terrain of subjectivity barely known at its beginning" (Habermas, 1991, p. 50). Subjectivity, then, was formed by a dialectical force: it was at one and the same time "the innermost core of the private… [yet] always already oriented to the audience" (Habermas, 1991, p. 49). Habermas refers to different media or spheres where publicity could take place, among which is the paper on which text could be written, newspapers, books, letter, and diaries. Such media changed "the relations between author, work, and public […] They became intimate mutual relationships between privatized individuals who were psychologically interested in what was 'human', in self-knowledge, and in empathy" (Habermas, 1991, p. 50). Later works have dealt more systematically with the relationship between the ledger and the diary and the rise of subjectivity (Aho, 2005; Basil, 1947; Chiapello, 2007; Gleeson-White, 2013; Heehs, 2013; Holton, 1983; Levy, 2014; Porter, 1997; Sangster, 2016; Soll, 2014; Urton, 2009).

Bookkeeping and diary-keeping are not so different as far as their method of creating new knowledge is concerned. Both bookkeeping and diary-keeping rendered data and information into a first-order objective knowledge about the world and a second-order subjective knowledge about their self. What was actually put into these media were data about financial transactions and daily occurrences, respectively. But because of how data were arranged, these media also gave rise to a new knowledge about the well-being of the business/self, which, in turn, gave rise to a new way of knowing the self. Epistemic media and its increasing centrality in individual and social life facilitated the development of modern subjectivity.

Underlying the link between media and subjectivity is a new epistemic sensibility, a new method for the self to form knowledge about itself: self-reflection. Such capacity emerges when an object is *reflected* upon media and is re-presented to the former to the point where this representation transforms the object into a subject. An exemplar media to facilitate such transformation is the mirror which turns one's gaze upon itself. Subjectivity emerges, *inter alia*, in the interconnection of humans and epistemic media: as people use media to record data about the world and about themselves, they are also transformed by a new kind of knowledge that these media create.

As aforementioned, the relationship between epistemic media and subjectivity is neither deterministic nor direct; there is another component at play here. What some epistemic media facilitate (and some don't) is self-reflection, a key sensibility in the emergence of critical knowledge about the self. It is this capacity, this space, opened up by critical knowledge about the self, which serves as the foundation for subjectivity. To clarify the particular nature of self-reflection or critical knowledge and its relations to the subjectivity, and in order to highlight the role of epistemic media in such endeavor, let me now turn to Habermas's critical sociology of knowledge.

Epistemic Media and Human Interest

In *Knowledge and Human Interests* (1972), Habermas offers a critical sociology of knowledge. At the time of its publication in 1968, knowledge was becoming an important axis in sociological theory (Castells, 2010; Mattelart, 2003; Stehr, 2001; Thrift, 2005; Webster, 2002). It was beginning to be understood as standing at the heart of a radical shift in the social structure of Western societies. This was a view shared by schools of diverse paradigmatic approaches and political affinities. The most notable sociologist to theorize the emerging centrality of knowledge in determining the social structure was Daniel Bell. A postindustrial society, where knowledge and information gain an axial role in the organization of society, sees the rise of a rationalized class of professionals and of a technocratic government, both bent on applying knowledge to solve political problems (Bell, 1999).

Bell's focus on a radical break in the social structure was coupled by other theories' focus on a radical break in social epistemology, brought about by the centrality of knowledge in society. Coming mostly from French post-structuralism, Lyotard (1984), Foucault (1994), Derrida (1974), and Baudrillard (1981) all undermined the hitherto *sine qua non* of knowledge, its representationally: the capacity of knowledge (in principle if not in reality) to correspond with reality. In their formulation, knowledge was becoming a central axis of the social to a point of overwhelming reality, losing its analytical distinction from power. Both approaches, then, posit knowledge as a new axis for sociability, but with very different sociological ramifications. Whereas Bell and other structuralists conceive knowledge as allowing the rationalization of society by making ideologies irrelevant – purifying politics from ideology – post-structuralists expressed deep disbelief in knowledge as a rationalizing agent, insisting on its impurity and interlacing with the political.

Habermas's intervention into the question of knowledge and society should be seen against this backdrop. Habermas sought to offer a *critical* theory of knowledge, which upholds knowledge as an agent of rationalization and at the same time account for its ability to transform reality toward a horizon of emancipation. How can knowledge be committed to both (scientific) "truth" and (political) "emancipation?" Habermas's solution is to suggest that historically human culture (in its Western variant, at least) has developed three different categories of knowledge and that these are inextricably linked with human interests. In other words, all knowledge is political; it inevitably operates within the contours of human ends. The choice of the word *interests* in the book's title is illuminating and makes for two different readings. Interest can refer to a sense of intellectual curiosity and a drive to understand reality; "knowledge for the sake of knowledge" (Habermas, 1972, p. 314). Such a reading would suggest that Habermas's book is concerned with what individuals and societies are interested in. Interest can also refer to having a stake at an issue, to standing to gain or lose from an issue. That would suggest Habermas's book refers to what individuals and societies have concern in or a stake at. The title could also mean both and suggest (as I think Habermas does) that what humans are interested in is inextricably linked with what serves their interests. It suggests that we cannot dissociate the history of knowledge from the political contours within which humans operate. To use a contemporaneous formulation, Habermas suggests that rather than ignoring or condemning the nexus of knowledge/power, it should rather be examined and theorized. And that's what Habermas sets out to do.

Habermas identifies three types of knowledge interests – i.e., reasons why humans are interested in gaining knowledge – each stemming from human existence and having come to be articulated in a particular type of scientific or scholarly inquiry. The first is a "technical interest", our species' survivalist interest in controlling and predicting our natural environment. This interest has given rise to the "empirical-analytic" sciences, mostly the natural sciences, but also streams in the social sciences that have been modeled after the natural sciences. This knowledge approaches nature and society as objects, which are governed by predictable regularities, and which can therefore be discovered by controlled methodologies (e.g., experiments), articulated into law-like theories, and even manipulated through intervention.

Second is a "practical interest", which involves the attempt to secure and expand the possibilities for mutual understanding in the conduct of life. This interest gives rise to the "cultural-hermeneutic" sciences, a type of knowledge that presupposes and articulates modes of personal and interpersonal understanding, which are oriented toward action. Such understanding is not "scientific" or "objective" in the common sense, but is part of the lifeworld and is expressed in the grammar of ordinary language. It is exercised in realms of knowledge such as history, anthropology, and parts of sociology. Both the empirical-analytic sciences and the cultural-hermeneutic sciences are academically established and constitute a hegemony of knowledge.

But Habermas wishes to go beyond this hegemony by pointing to another deep-rooted human interest, which has given rise to another form of knowledge. This is the "emancipatory interest" of reason to overcome (externally imposed) dogmatism, (internally induced) compulsion, and (interpersonal and social) domination. The emancipatory interest gives rise to critical knowledge. Critical knowledge has a few defining features that Habermas would go on to examine in later works, most famously in *The Theory of Communicative Action* (Habermas, 1985). Particularly crucial to our discussion is the *reflexive* character of critical knowledge, i.e., the central role of the knower in the creation of knowledge. Creating critical knowledge about human beings (as social, anthropological, or psychological begins) is a *praxis* which requires the participation of the objects of that knowledge, i.e., human beings. Critical, emancipatory knowledge involves subjectivity as both a precondition and a product. Critical knowledge can only emerge with the involvement of subjectivity; subjectivity, in turn, can only emerge with critical knowledge.

With the notion of critical knowledge, Habermas sought to offer a category of knowledge, which describes reality and the conditions under which this reality comes about. Such knowledge can then serve to inform actions needed in order to change these conditions. It is therefore at once both objective and subjective. As McCarthy notes in the introduction to Habermas's *On the Logic of the Social Sciences*, Habermas "finds that the attempt to conceive of the social system as a functional complex of institutions in which cultural patterns are made normatively binding for action" – a description corresponding more or less to Talcott Parsons's by-then hegemonic social theory – "does furnish us with important tools for analyzing objective interconnections of action; but it suffers from a short-circuiting of the hermeneutic and critical dimensions of social analysis" (Habermas, 1988, p. viii). In other words, such theory excludes the communicative, subjective, and intersubjective dimensions of society, where actors reflect upon their action.

With critical knowledge, Habermas calls for the uncovering of that which not-yet-is and may never be unless we notice it and made knowledge about it explicit. This is the Schrödinger's cat of the social and the cultural. And whether we find out the cat is dead or alive depends on our epistemology, i.e., our understanding of what knowing is:

> In the framework of action theory [*à la* Parsons], motives for action are harmonized with institutional values... We may assume, however, that repressed needs which are not absorbed into social roles, transformed into motivations, and sanctioned, nevertheless have their interpretations.
>
> (Habermas, 1988, p. viii)

One of these cats, which can hardly be noticed by action theory, is subjectivity, an elusive construct which is always in the making and which only through self-reflection can gain access to critical knowledge, which, in turn, will materialize its emancipatory interests.

The moment we start to ask ourselves about our self, we also change it. One of the paradigmatic methodical ways to make that inquiry in the 20th century has been psychoanalysis. Habermas considers psychoanalysis as an exemplar of critical knowledge serving an emancipatory interest (along with Marxism and Critical Theory, of which he was part). Psychoanalysis is particularly illustrative for our inquiry of epistemic media, as it too involves an individual seeking to learn about herself through formalized methodical means. The plurality and diversity of these means is obviously immense, and I wish to focus here on one aspect which Habermas finds cardinal to the creation of critical knowledge: self-reflection, i.e., the involvement of the subject in creating knowledge about itself.

Self-Reflection in Psychoanalysis

Psychoanalysis may be seen as akin to the natural science in its objectivity and scienticity. This was indeed the position taken by Freud himself who sought to "elevate" psychoanalysis into a real science, making its knowledge instrumental, in Habermas's terms. Alternatively, says Habermas, psychoanalysis may seem to produce a special form of interpretation, making its knowledge practical. But Habermas seeks to show the unique character of psychoanalytic knowledge, not merely as instrumental and practical but as critical as well. Let us think about interpreting a dream, as an example. While it may seem that the interpretive effort of the analyst is akin to that of the philologist interpreting a text, Habermas insists that the psychoanalyst's work "requires a specifically expanded hermeneutics, one that, in contrast to the usual method of interpretation in the cultural sciences, takes into account a new dimension" (Habermas, 1972, p. 215), like that of the dream's author. Habermas refers to that as "methodical self-reflection" (Habermas, 1972, p. 214).

Like psychoanalysis, cultural interpretation too may take interest in the interpretation offered by the text's author. But cultural interpretation differs from psychoanalysis, "in that it takes the intentional structure of subjective consciousness [i.e. the author's interpretation] as the ultimate experiential basis in the process of appropriating objective mind" (Habermas, 1972, p. 216). Hermeneutic interpretation goes as deep as the intentions of the author; "psychoanalytic interpretation, in contrast, is not directed at meaning structures in the dimension of what is consciously intended" (Habermas, 1972, pp. 216–217); rather, it seeks to mobilize the consciousness of the subject in order to interpret the dream. The interpretive challenge of psychoanalysis is greater as it assumes that the text to be interpreted is corrupted, and that this corruption is itself key for interpretation. The omissions and distortions of the dream, as it is told by the subject, "have a systemic role and function. For the symbolic structures that psychoanalysis seeks to comprehend are corrupted by the impact of internal condition" (Habermas, 1972, p. 217).

Achieving critical knowledge about the self poses an inherent challenge: subjects need to use reason to uncover that which their unreason affects. "Psychoanalytic interpretation is concerned with those connections of symbols in which a subject deceives itself about itself" (Habermas, 1972, p. 218). The dreamer is put in a difficult epistemic position: to be the detective that outsmarts the deceiver and be both at the same time. Dreams, says Habermas, "document the latent content of a portion of the author's orientations that has become inaccessible to him and alienated from him and yet belongs to him nevertheless" (Habermas, 1972, p. 218). This duality – a part of the self being inaccessible to another part, but also integral to its whole – is also the key for gaining self-knowledge. In other words, this duality creates a puzzle, but it also signals the solution to the puzzle: self-reflection.

Self-reflection, then, assumes a subject duality, a subject which is able to at once make sense and produce meaningful utterances (such as a dream) and be oblivious of their meaning: "after waking, the subject, who is still in some way identical with the author of the dream, no longer understands his creation" (Habermas, 1972, p. 219). The interpretation of dreams, then, is not a simple reading of the text but "always the model for the illumination of pathologically distorted meaning structures" (Habermas, 1972, p. 220). While the analyst is supposed to strictly take the attitude of the interpreter, her own hermeneutic view does not suffice, "For dreams are among those texts that confront the author himself as alienated and incomprehensible" (Habermas, 1972, p. 220). For that reason:

> the technique of dream interpretation goes beyond the art of hermeneutics insofar as it must grasp not only the meaning of a possibly distorted text, but the meaning of the text distortion itself, that is the transformation of a latent dream thought into the manifest dream.
>
> (Habermas, 1972, p. 220)

Reflection, then, is key to psychoanalytic knowledge:

> Seen from the analyst's perspective, it remains mere knowledge 'for us', until its communication turns into enlightenment—that is, into knowledge 'for it', for the patient's consciousness: 'On that particular matter our knowledge will then have become his knowledge as well.'
>
> (Habermas, 1972, pp. 230–231)

The relations between subjectivity and knowledge are dialectical and mediated by self-reflection. As self-reflection joins the process of knowledge production, the ontological status of knowledge changes as well; it no longer reflects merely objective reality but also the subjective interpretation of that reality, which embodies emancipatory interests. Habermas, therefore, considers self-reflection as an *experience*, which fuses knowledge and praxis:

> the experience of the emancipatory power of reflection, which the subject experiences in itself to the extent that it becomes transparent to itself in the history of its genesis. The experience of reflection articulates itself substantially in the concept of a self-formative process.
>
> (Habermas, 1972, p. 197)

To the extent that knowledge is transparent to the subject through self-reflection, it also partakes in its genesis or self-formation. This makes critical knowledge generative and transformative to the subject:

> [It] take[s] into account that information about lawlike connections sets off a process of reflection in the consciousness of those

whom the laws are about. Thus the level of unreflected consciousness, which is one of the initial conditions of such laws, can be transformed. Of course, to this end a critically mediated knowledge of laws cannot through reflection alone render a law itself inoperative, but it can render it inapplicable.

(Habermas, 1972, p. 310)

Algorithmic Knowledge and Human Interest

If knowledge of the self was key to the construction of modern subjectivity and if epistemic media were instrumental in that endeavor, then we might expect digital media to be the pinnacle of that trend, as the creation of knowledge is so central to their operating rationale. Indeed, creating knowledge about users is a quintessential feature of digital media, at least since the arrival of Web 2.0. The very notion of Web 2.0, first emerging from industry and later entering academic discourse as well, signals the transformation of the web from a repository of information into a machine for monitoring and processing users' data (Fisher, 2017). A key novelty of Web 2.0 was personalization, the ability to render users' data into knowledge about them in order to tailor personal content for them.

The next phase in the development of the web as a knowing machine was platformization (van Dijck, Poell, & de Waal, 2018). First came social networking sites, later social media, and finally platformization became the paradigmatic organizing form for the web (Srnicek, 2016). Platformization entails the ability to collect immense quantities and varieties of data from multiple sources, process them in real time, and create knowledge which is at once system-wide and personalized (Helmond, 2015). The social graph of Facebook, personalized recommendations of Netflix, and driving directions of Waze, to name a few examples, are premised on the epistemic character of digital media.

As digital media create knowledge about users, this knowledge also informs users' knowledge about themselves. Algorithmic knowledge informs the self-knowledge of users both directly and indirectly. Indirectly, users inevitably know that they are being monitored by digital media and that what they encounter in their interactions with these machines reflects how these media perceive them based on the data that their behavior produces (Bucher, 2012). At least to some extent, and with a necessary grain of salt, users see a link between recommendations for books (on Amazon), movies (on Netflix), friends (on Facebook) on the one hand, and their behavior on these platforms on the other hand. It is not necessarily a naïve stance and users may object to being interpellated (or "stigmatized") by the algorithm ("why Alibaba keeps offering me home improvement products? I am uninterested in that") (Siles, Espinoza-Rojas, Naranjo, & Tristán, 2019). But the idea of creating a correlation is clear: platforms are using algorithms in order to create knowledge about their users. This experience of digital platforms as mirrors of ourselves is almost inescapable, to the extent that if users have any digital literacy, they know that what they encounter online reflects how the platform perceives them (Afriat et al., 2020).

There is also a more direct way by which digital media creates knowledge about the self for the self through all sorts of voluntary and quasi-voluntary quantification devices. Voluntarily, these are mostly platforms relating to the quantified self, a conscious and systematic attempt by users to collect personal data and render it into algorithmic knowledge, predominantly applications that monitor health and well-being (Lupton, 2016; Ruckenstein & Pantzar, 2015). There are also platforms that reflect algorithmic knowledge to users about their activities (Kennedy & Hill, 2018; Kennedy & Moss, 2015). This can be thought of as quasi-voluntary, as this self-quantification is not necessarily called for by the user.

With digital media, we can therefore note an undisputable rise of mediated knowledge about the self. Indeed, this explosion of information and its popularization has led to new forms of representation which account for the democratization of knowledge about the self, i.e., an attempt to make this knowledge accessible to lay people. An epitome of that has been the rise of data visualization and infographics (Drucker, 2020; Roski, Bo-Linn, & Andrews, 2014). This indicates the tremendous efforts made by digital platforms to communicate the epistemic ability of data and algorithms and to make the knowledge they produce into a common currency for everyday life and public culture. That and more, contrary to previous epistemic media which were immobile, digital platforms are used on mobile devices, and users' interaction with them is frequent, ubiquitous, and intimate.

So how can we understand the knowledge that digital media create about the self? Algorithmic systems are notoriously opaque; how algorithms actually turn data into knowledge is hard to ascertain. This is not only because of intellectual property and concerns over secrecy, but also because the epistemology of algorithms is un-theorized. Engineers know better how to build algorithms and how to evaluate their practical merit (e.g., improving prediction through A/B testing) than to explain the workings of a particular algorithmic device due to its complexity.

Analytically speaking, the way that algorithms create knowledge about users is quite similar to traditional epistemic media. I have outlined above the unique features which make a media form and a media practice epistemic, i.e., able to create new knowledge about the self: (i) real-time recording of (ii) data (iii) over time (iv) by a particular individual, which (v) results in new knowledge. Digital media subscribe to this generative form in many respects, *missing one crucial feature: the incorporation of self-reflection.* What in traditional epistemic media needs to be recorded becomes a direct footprint of behavior in digital media. If events once needed to be transferred from their happening in the phenomenal world to a media form, in the case of digital platforms events are already part of the system. Every event is registered as data and every data point is multiplied by metadata.

Interestingly, the algorithmic episteme share many common assumptions with the psychoanalytic episteme. Both epistemes question the idea that reason has unmediated access to all facets of the self, such as wants. Digital media solves this problem by bypassing what people claim to want or claim their taste to be, and instead gauging their wants and taste through data derived from their actions. Overcoming these obstacles to self-understanding is based on dataism, a theology of data which sees it as the basic building block for knowledge, and sees data – specifically the data that individuals produce while engaging with digital technology – as comprising the "source code" of humanness (van Dijck, 2014). Nicholas Rose conceptualizes the theology of neuroscience which sees neural activity similarly (Rose & Abi-Rached, 2013). In this case, however, the building blocks are not naturally occurring neuroelectrical charges, but rather digital data registered as indicators of behavior (Zuboff, 2015).

The key distinction pertains to the role that psychoanalysis nevertheless assigns to self in the process of self-knowledge. This distinction stems from a radically different conception of the self. Psychoanalysis offers critical knowledge about the self by creating a space between an actually existing self and an emancipated self as abstract, theoretical, even utopian construct. Psychoanalysis sees in the knowledge about the self a means to uncover that which hinders human freedom, and thus a means to point toward a quasi-transcendental move toward emancipation. Psychoanalytic knowledge about the self, therefore, opens up a space for facets of the self that do not yet show themselves in the actually existing self. Such a self can demarcate a utopian horizon toward which it can be directed. Hence, psychoanalysis could take the observed, behavioral aspects of the self as partial and as merely a starting point. An observed behavior could be interpreted by the self as a sign of anxiety, the roots of which may be uncovered, and through therapy, the behavior may be transformed.

Such a progressive move requires a few important elements missing from the algorithmic episteme, elements which make the knowledge it creates about the self inherently uncritical. I have focused in this article on one such element: self-reflection. While it is true that algorithms also reflect (just like a therapist) facets of the self that of which the self may be unaware or even resistant, it excludes the self from the process of discovery, as this is done away from its sight and understanding. To accomplish self-reflection requires another component missing from the algorithmic episteme: natural language. Language allows self-reflection, it allows reason to reflect and examine the self, and, in turn, transform the conditions of possibility of observed behavior. Self-reflection allows us, for example, to behave anxiously and at the same time identify that behavior as anxiety and as hurtful to self or others. In other words, an imagined emancipatory self, which does not yet exist, can nevertheless outline a path for the self to walk in and become that. This can only be achieved through language, interpretation, and self-reflection. It is precisely in that sense that Habermas insists that psychoanalysis is not a positivist science like the natural science, but actually an exemplar of critical theory which has an interest in (and a capacity to create) knowledge, which at one and the same time describes reality and allows the subject to move toward a desired reality with the aid of reason.

The algorithmic episteme represents a collapse of that constructive space between theory of the self and the performative, actually existing self, as well as an impossibility to communicate in natural language. Algorithms paint a much more monolithic self: an acting or behaving self. It is a self devoid of leverage for critique, anchored much more firmly in the reality principle, in that which exists in a given time in the form of performative data. It is knowledge that relegates any other facets from the perception of the self, facets which can only be manifested through language (Hildebrandt, 2019; Rouvroy, 2013; Rouvroy & Stiegler, 2016).

Conclusion

Subjectivity has been a promise, born in the Enlightenment, to expand the realm of freedom from internal impulses and external coercion. Arguably, this promise was never – and could never be – materialized to the fullest. But it nevertheless gave a horizon for what human freedom might mean. Subjectivity was seen not as an ontology of human existence to be unveiled, but as a project worthy of achieving. And epistemic media have been seen as instruments to bring it about by offering a new theater where self-reflection can thrive and bring about a new kind of knowledge about the self.

Digital media now offer a new model of knowledge about the self, based on the algorithmic processing of big data gathered mostly by using this very media. For the last few centuries, self-reflection has been the cornerstone of subjectivity, which was, in turn, a precondition for freedom. By demoting self-reflection, digital media and algorithmic knowledge redefine what self-knowledge means and, in turn, redefine subjectivity. What is in fact the promise of freedom underlying algorithmic knowledge? If the dictum *know thyself* promised a route for a more emancipated subjectivity, what kind of freedom is promised by algorithms knowing you?

Acknowledgement

This chapter was previously published as a journal article in Critical Sociology OnlineFirst, Sept 22, 2021. Permission for reprint has been duly obtained from publisher.

References

Afriat, H., Dvir-Gvirsman, S., Tsuriel, K., & Ivan, L. (2020). "This is capitalism. It is not illegal": Users' attitudes toward institutional privacy following the Cambridge Analytica scandal. *Information Society, 37*(2), 115–127. https://Doi.org/10.1080/01972243.2020.1870596

Aho, J. (2005). *Confession and bookkeeping: The religious, moral, and rhetorical roots of modern accounting.* Albany: State University of New York Press.

Andrejevic, M. (2012). Exploitation in the data mine. In C. Fuchs, K. Boersma, A. Albrechtslund, & M. Sandoval (Eds.), *Internet and surveillance: The challenges of Web 2.0 and social media* (pp. 71–88). New York: Routledge.

Basil, Y. (1947). Notes on the origin of double-entry bookkeeping. *The Accounting Review, 22*(3), 263–272.

Baudrillard, J. (1981). *For a critique of the political economy of the sign.* St. Louis: Telos Press.

Bell, D. (1999). *The coming of post-industrial society: A venture in social forecasting.* New York: Basic books.

Blair, A. M. (2011). *Too much to know: Managing scholarly information before the modern age.* New Haven: Yale University Press.

Bucher, T. (2012). Want to be on the top? Algorithmic power and the threat of invisibility on Facebook. *New Media and Society, 14*(7), 1164–1180.

Burke, P. (2000). *Social history of knowledge: From Guthenberg to Diderot.* Cambridge: Polity.

Casasanto, D., Jasmin, K., Brookshire, G., Gijssels, T. (2014). The QWERTY Effect: How typing shapes word meanings and baby names. In P. Bello, M. Guarini, M. McShane, & B. Scassellati (Eds.), *Proceedings of the 36th Annual Conference of the Cognitive Science Society* (pp. 296–301). Austin, TX: Cognitive Science Society.

Castells, M. (2010). *The information age: Economy, society and culture.* Cambridge, MA and Oxford: Blackwell.

Chiapello, E. (2007). Accounting and the birth of the notion of capitalism. *Critical Perspectives on Accounting*, 18: 263–296.

Clanchy, M. (2013). *From memory to written record: England 1066-1307* (3rd ed.). Oxford: Wiley-Blackwell.

Derrida, J. (1974). *Of grammatology.* Baltimore, MD: Johns Hopkins University Press.

Drucker, J. (2020). *Visualization and interpretation: Humanistic approaches to display.* Cambridge, MA: MIT Press.

Fisher, Eran. (2015). Audience labour in social media: Lessons from the political economy of the internet. In Nelly Elias, Galit Nimrod, Zvi Reich, & Amit Schejter (Eds), *Media in Transition* (pp. 105–126), Tel Aviv: Tzivonim [in Hebrew].

Fisher, E. (2017). When information wanted to be free: Discursive bifurcation of information and the origins of Web 2.0. *Information Society*, 34(1): 40–48.

Foucault, M. (1994). *The order of things: An archeology of human sciences.* New York: Vintage Books.

Garcia, D., & Strohmaier, M. (2016). The QWERTY effect on the web. *25th International World Wide Web Conference, WWW 2016.* https://doi.org/10.1145/2872427.2883019

Gitelman, L. (2014). *Paper knowledge : Toward a media history of documents.* Durham, NC: Duke University Press.

Gleeson-White, J. (2013). *Double entry : How the merchants of Venice created modern finance.* New York: W.W. Norton & Company.

Goody, J. (1977). *The domestication of the savage mind.* Cambridge: Cambridge University Press.

Goody, J. (1986). *The logic of writing and the organization of society.* Cambridge: Cambridge University Press.

Habermas, J. (1972). *Knowledge and human interests.* Boston, MA: Beacon Press.

Habermas, J. (1985). *The theory of communicative action.* Boston, MA: Beacon Press.

Habermas, J. (1988). *On the logic of the social sciences.* Cambridge MA: MIT Press.

Habermas, J. (1991). *The structural transformation of the public sphere: An inquiry into a category of Bourgeois society.* Cambridge, MA: MIT Press.

Hankins, T. L. (1985). *Science and the enlightenment.* Cambridge: Cambridge University Press.

Havelock, E. (1988). *The muse learns to write: Reflections on orality and literacy from antiquity to the present.* New Haven: Yale University Press.

Heehs, P. (2013). *Writing the self: Diaries, memoirs, and the history of the self.* London: Bloomsbury.

Heesen, A. Te. (2000). Boxes in nature. *Studies in history and philosophy of science Part A, 31*(3), 381–403. https://doi.org/10.1016/s0039-3681(00)00017-0

Helmond, A. (2015). The platformization of the web: Making web data platform ready. *Social Media and Society, 1*(2). https://doi.org/10.1177/2056305115603080

Hildebrandt, M. (2019). Privacy as protection of the incomputable self: From agnostic to agonistic machine learning. *Theoretical Inquiries in Law, 20*(1), 83–121. https://doi.org/10.1515/til-2019-0004

Holton, R. J. (1983). Max Weber, "Rational Capitalism," and renaissance Italy: A critique of Cohen. *American Journal of Sociology, 89*(1), 166–180. https://doi.org/10.1086/227837

Houston, K. (2016). *The book: A cover-to-cover exploration of the most powerful object of our time.* New York: W. W. Norton & Company.

Innis, H. A. (1995). *The bias of communication.* Toronto: University of Toronto Press.

Jasmin, K., & Casasanto, D. (2012). The QWERTY effect: How typing shapes the meanings of words. *Psychonomic Bulletin and Review,* (19), 499–504. https://doi.org/10.3758/s13423-012-0229-7

Kafka, B. (2012). *The demon of writing: Powers and failures of paperwork.* New York: Zone Books.

Kelly, T. F. (2019). *The role of the scroll: An illustrated introduction to scrolls in the middle ages.* New York: W. W. Norton & Company.

Kennedy, H., & Hill, R.L. (2018). The feeling of numbers: Emotions in everyday engagements with data and their visualisation. *Sociology.* 52(*4*), 830–848. doi:10.1177/0038038516674675

Kennedy, H., & Moss, G. (2015). Known or knowing publics? Social media data mining and the question of public agency. *Big Data & Society, 2*(2), 205395171561114. https://doi.org/10.1177/2053951715611145

Kessler, F., Chateau, D., & Moure, J. (2018). The screen and the concept of dispositif–A dialogue. In *Screens.* https://doi.org/10.1515/9789048531691-023

Kirschenbaum, M. (2016). *Track changes: A literary history of word processing.* Cambridge, MA: Belknap Press.

Kittler, F. (1992). *Discourse networks, 1800/1900.* Stanford: Stanford University Press.

Kittler, F. (1999). *Gramophone, film, typewriter.* Stanford: Stanford University Press.

Knorr Cetina, K. (1999). *Epistemic cultures: How the sciences make knowledge.* Cambridge, MA: Harvard University Press.

Krajewski, M. (2011). *Paper machines: About cards & catalogs, 1548-1929.* Cambridge, MA: MIT Press.

Levy, J. (2014). Accounting for profit and the history of capital. *Critical Historical Studies, 1*(2), 171–214. https://doi.org/10.1086/677977

Lupton, D. (2016). *The quantified self.* Malden, MA: Polity Press.

Lyotard, J. F. (1984). *The postmodern condition: A report on knowledge.* Minneapolis: University of Minnesota Press.

MacKenzie, D. (1996). *Knowing machines: Essays on technological change.* Cambridge, MA: MIT Press.

Mak, B. (2012). *How the page matters.* Toronto: University of Toronto Press.

Mattelart, A. (2003). *The information society: An introduction.* Thousand Oaks, CA: Sage.

McLuhan, M. (1994). *Understanding media: The extensions of man.* Boston, MA: MIT Press.

McLuhan, M. (2011). *The Gutenberg galaxy.* Toronto: University of Toronto Press.

Müller-Wille, S., & Charmantier, I. (2012). Lists as research technologies. *ISIS.* https://doi.org/10.1086/669048

Ong, W. J. (1982). *Orality and literacy: The technologizing of the word.* London and New York: Routledge.

Peters, J. D. (2015). *The marvelous clouds: Toward a philosophy of elemental media.* Chicago: University of Chicago Press.

Porter, R. (1997). *Rewriting the self: Histories from the middle ages to the present.* London: Routledge.

Postman, N. (1993). *Technopoly: The surrender of culture to technology.* New York: Vintage Books.

Postman, N. (2005). *Amusing ourselves to death: Public discourse in the age of show business.* New York: Penguin Books.

Rose, N., & Abi-Rached, J. (2013). *Neuro: The new brain sciences and the management of the mind.* Princeton: Princeton University Press.

Roski, J., Bo-Linn, G. W., & Andrews, T. A. (2014). Creating value in health care through big data: Opportunities and policy implications. *Health Affairs, 33*(7), 1115–1122. https://doi.org/10.1377/hlthaff.2014.0147

Rossiter, N. (2016). *Software, infrastructure, labor: A media theory of logistical nightmares.* London: Routledge.

Rouvroy, A. (2013). The end(s) of critique: Data behaviourism versus due process. In Hildebrandt, M. & de Vries, K. (Eds.), *Privacy due process and the computational turn: The philosophy of law meets the philosophy of technology* (pp. 143–168). London: Routledge. https://doi.org/10.4324/9780203427644.

Rouvroy, A., & Stiegler, B. (2016). The digital regime of truth : From the algorithmic governmentality to a new rule of law *. *Online Journal of Philosophy, 3,* 6–29.

Ruckenstein, M., & Pantzar, M. (2015). Beyond the quantified self: Thematic exploration of a dataistic paradigm. *New Media & Society, 19*(3), 401–418. https://doi.org/10.1177/1461444815609081

Sangster, A. (2016). The genesis of double entry bookkeeping. *Accounting Review, 91*(1), 299–315. https://doi.org/10.2308/accr-51115

Scholz, T. (2013). *Digital labour: The internet as playground and factory.* New York: Routledge.

Siles, I., Espinoza-Rojas, J., Naranjo, A., & Tristán, M. F. (2019). The mutual domestication of users and algorithmic recommendations on

Netflix. *Communication, Culture and Critique*, 12(4), 499–518. https://doi.org/10.1093/ccc/tcz025

Soll, J. (2014). *The reckoning : Financial accountability and the rise and fall of nations*. New York: Basic Books.

Srnicek, N. (2016). *Platform capitalism*. Cambridge: Polity Press.

Stehr, N. (2001). *The fragility of modern societies: Knowledge and risk in the information age*. Thousand Oaks, CA: Sage.

Thrift, N. (2005). *Knowing capitalism*. London: Sage.

Urton, G. (2009). Sin, confession, and the arts of book- and cord-keeping: An intercontinental and transcultural exploration of accounting and governmentality. *Comparative Studies in Society and History 51*(4), 801–831. https://doi.org/10.1017/S0010417509990144

van Dijck, J. (2014). Datafication, dataism and dataveillance: Big Data between scientific paradigm and ideology. *Surveillance and Society, 12*(2), 197–208.

van Dijck, J., Poell, T., & de Waal, M. (2018). *The platform society: Public values in a connective world*. Oxford: Oxford University Press.

Vismann, C. (2008). *Files: Law and media technology*. Stanford: Stanford University Press.

Weber, M. (1958). *The protestant ethic and the spirit of capitalism*. New York: Scribners.

Webster, F. (2002). *Theories of the information society*. London: Routledge.

Young, L. C. (2015). Cultural techniques and logistical media: Tuning German and Anglo-American media studies. *M/C Journal, 18*(2). https://doi.org/10.5204/mcj.961

Zuboff, S. (2015). Big other: Surveillance capitalism and the prospects of an information civilization. *Journal of Information Technology, 30*(1), 75–89. https://doi.org/10.1057/jit.2015.5

Zuboff, S. (2020). *The age of surveillance capitalism: The fight for a human future at the new frontier of power*. New York: PublicAffairs.

2 Algorithms, Conventions and New Regulation Processes

Rainer Diaz-Bone and Simon Schrör

Introduction: Algorithmic Governance

Contemporary societies are data worlds. Digital devices, software and the Internet transform individuals' lifeworlds, personal communication, the economy (i.e., production processes, distribution and consumption), banking and credit, health care and health care insurance, public and private transport, law and the judicial system, policing and surveillance, social media and mass media and other private as well as public spheres into computerized realities and digital data. This transformation is grasped with notions (and buzz words) such as "datafication", "data revolution" or "big data" (Mayer-Schönberger and Cukier, 2013; Kitchin, 2014; Mejias and Couldry, 2019; Peeters and Schuilenburg, 2021). Although many user interfaces and representations on displays of digital devices (as smart phones, wearables, notebooks) are organized and offered in a non-numeric visual form (as images), the underlying data form is numerical. Nowadays, huge amounts of numerical data are generated, stored and analyzed mainly by big Internet companies, who detect behavioral patterns and exploit these to gain profits (Mayer-Schönberger and Cukier, 2013). In many countries, national security agencies gather data to track citizens' activities or to detect crime (*The Economist*, 2016; Botsman, 2017).

The notion of "big data" was originally invented to label amounts of data, which can no longer be stored on single computers ("volume"), which are produced and analyzed continuously ("velocity") and which vary in data formats ("variety"; Lazer and Radford, 2017). The notion of big data has become a present marker in public debates for utopian perspectives of data-driven innovations and economic progress (Mayer-Schönberger and Cukier, 2013; Mayer-Schönberger and Ramge, 2018) as well as for dystopian perspectives of surveillance and the control of individual behavior (Zuboff, 2019).

DOI: 10.4324/9781003173427-2

Related to notions as big data is the term algorithm, which has long been established in computer sciences. In fact, algorithms are "ordinary" parts of contemporary ways of living; they are ubiquitous in digitized societies. "Digital technology is enabled as much by its hardware, the physical components that make up computers and digital devices, as by its software, the programs that run on it. The backbone of programs are the algorithms that they implement" (Louridas, 2020: xiv).[1]

However, algorithms have become an issue in the social sciences, but also as a public discourse element too (Steiner, 2012; Pasquale, 2015; Beer, 2016, 2017; O'Neil, 2016; Eubanks, 2017; Burrell and Fourcade, 2021). The reason is that the power of big data unfolds only when it can be accessed by computer networks, which apply algorithms to detect patterns, and to automatically generate evaluations, predictions as well as decisions. More and more algorithms are applied to make important decisions, which affect everybody's everyday life. And many of these decisions can have negative and illegitimate effects, promote different forms of social inequality and result in unfair life chances (Fourcade and Healy, 2013; Eubanks, 2017; O'Neil, 2016). And it is this combination of big data and algorithms which enables its outreach of power effects to more and more domains and the emergence of new governance effects and governance forms:

We are living in the midst of a significant transformation of our lives, and while it is an incredible time and place to be in, we must be wary of the effects that come along with it. Mind-boggling amounts of data are generated regarding our daily actions with algorithms processing and acting upon these data to make decisions that manage, control, and nudge our behavior in everyday life. The use of algorithms not only expands the possibilities of current control and surveillance, but also introduces a new paradigm characterized by an increased rationality of governance, a shift in the functioning of power, and closure of decision-making procedures. We can refer to this by using the term 'algorithmic governance' – the replacement of human, legible and accountable judgements with 'black-box' algorithms [...]. Algorithmic governance is central to the functioning of public and private organizations. For instance, police forces use them to predict where, when and by whom crimes are more likely to be committed [...]. In criminal justice, algorithms are used to predict future dangerousness of defendants and convicts [...]. Marketeers use algorithms to analyze consumer audiences from online search queries, credit card purchase data, and behavioral data […]. Government agencies are turning towards algorithms to, among other things, identify welfare fraud, deliver public services, allocate regulatory oversight resources, and assess risks in child protection […]. Taken together, algorithms, machine learning and artificial intelligence form the new digital infrastructure of our society.

(Peeters and Schuilenburg, 2021: 1/3/4)[2]

It is evident that algorithms are based on norms and normative decisions, on programmers' values and principles, how to quantify and how to categorize events, persons or objects (Desrosières, 2008; O'Neil, 2016). As Peeters and Schuilenburg (2021: 4) emphasize, "algorithms can only exist in a stable environment of standardized codes and classifications", categories and quantifications are their "input" and (in many applications) also their "output". Algorithmic governance therefore can be conceived of as the power to classify and quantify persons, objects and events on the basis of social conventions how to categorize and to quantify. These classifications and quantifications are articulated by different words such as "scoring", "sorting", "ranking", "rating", "status determination", "clustering", "risk assessments" etc., and they all imply an evaluative and valorizing effect. These classifications and quantifications are in fact measurements, which are themselves built up on norms, values and – more broadly conceived – on societal rationalities and institutional logics. And algorithms themselves entail normative decisions and value-based criteria (as criteria, how to optimize or when to end the calculation).[3] This is not an argument to discredit or to dismiss measurements and algorithms, which both are inevitable in modern societies. But the argument points to the need to scrutinize the link between measurements, algorithms and values as well as its effects.

For sociology, the analysis of power effects, released and advanced by datafication, measurement and algorithms is of core importance – as notions like "social power of algorithms" (Beer, 2017) or "algorithmic power" (Lash, 2007; Peeters and Schuilenburg, 2021) highlight. But different additional positions and perspectives should be included in the analysis of the relation between datafication, measurement, algorithms on one side and society, power effects and governance on the other side. (1) It is important not to restrict the analysis to the power effects only, but to open the black box of measurement and algorithmic calculation itself. (2) Also, sociological analysis has to recognize the plurality of data worlds, of normative orders and value systems, which influence datafication, measurement and algorithmic governance. (3)

Therefore, it is important not to assume coherent power effects and to include non-intended and countervailing power effects, resistance and social critique too. (4) Finally, if processes of datafication and algorithms are to be evaluated from a sociological point of view, there is a need to relate them to collective action and to common goods and to ask how datafication and algorithms enhance capacities and enable agency to approach social problems, to improve living conditions as well as social participation and in general to advance societies.

In this contribution, the black box of these measurements is conceptually approached by relying on the institutionalist approach of *economics and sociology of conventions* (EC/SC). Also, this approach offers a pluralist perspective on data worlds, in which algorithms are differently developed, evaluated and applied.

In the next section ("Economics of Convention – Quantification, Algorithms and the Common Good"), the approach of EC/SC is introduced. Then the notion of data worlds is introduced ("The Plurality of Data Worlds and Data Regulation"). These worlds allow a differentiation that enables an analysis framework for algorithmic regulations to be developed ("Analyzing Algorithmic Regulations: Critique in Situations of Uncertainty"). Finally, the contribution applies the conventionalist framework to different examples of algorithmic norm setting and enforcement ("New Regulators – New Perspectives on Regulatory Processes").

Economics of Convention – Quantification, Algorithms and the Common Good

EC/SC was originally developed in France in the analysis of socio-economic categories and official statistics but spread out to become an interdisciplinary and international neopragmatist institutional approach (Storper and Salais, 1997; Boltanski and Thévenot, 2006; Eymard-Duvernay, 2006a, 2006b; Diaz-Bone and Salais, 2011; Diaz-Bone, 2018). The most widely known model of conventions was worked out by Luc Boltanski and Laurent Thévenot (2006), who identified the industrial convention, the market convention, the domestic convention, the convention of renown and the convention of inspiration. These conventions are deeper logics of quality assessment, but also for the critique and justification of worth. One neopragmatist core element is EC/SC's awareness of the link between facts and values, which is the link between norms and measurements (Desrosières, 2008, 2014; Diaz-Bone, 2016, 2017, 2019; Diaz-Bone and Didier, 2016; Diaz-Bone and Horvath, 2021). Measurements are therefore not impartial representations of a foregoing reality. Conventions are not understood as customs or traditions, but as institutional logic on how to interpret, evaluate and valuate (or valorize) persons, objects and events. As the convention theorist Alain Desrosières (2008: 10) stated: "to quantify is to implement a convention and then to measure". It is these measurement conventions which bring in the link between facts and values. EC/SC has argued that convention-based measurements can be evaluated by studying how they enable measurements, which enable collective action aiming for a common good. Measurement conventions are not only agreements about measurement procedures, but as Figure 2.1 shows, they are also agreements about the ontologies of what is to be measured, i.e., entities to be classified or to be quantified (Centemeri, 2012).

For EC/SC, measurement conventions are embedded in statistical chains, which are built by situations, in which different actors are involved in the production of data (Desrosières, 2000, 2009, 2011). Statistical chains (or statistical production chains) are characterized by a division of labor and can be burdened by differently applied conventions, which are mobilized by different actors. The notion of algorithm is different to the notion of statistical chains at first glance, because algorithms are built up by sets of calculative steps to proceed a designed task. Statistical chains can also be conceived of a series of steps, but in many cases, the whole chain cannot be planned and governed by one rational or one actor only and the chain is distributed (Diaz-Bone, 2016, 2017). But, as Dourish (2016) has argued, the elements or calculative steps of algorithms can be distributed too. Kitchin (2017) has pointed to the fact that algorithms are linked to other algorithms and

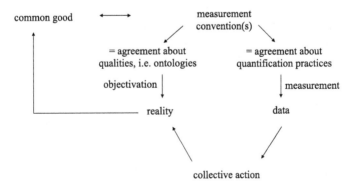

Figure 2.1 Measurement conventions.

build up "algorithm systems". All in all, the consequence is that data and algorithm-based data analysis is distributed in networks of computers, organizations and persons – as in many big data analyses. This way, calculative changes, incoherencies and problems of data quality and adequacies can emerge in algorithmic procedures too.

The Plurality of Data Worlds and Data Regulation

Another pragmatist core notion is that of "worlds". In EC/SC, this notion is applied to the plurality of "data worlds" (Diaz-Bone et al., 2020; Diaz-Bone and Horvath, 2021). In these data worlds different orders of worth and quality conventions (Boltanski and Thévenot, 2006) are combined and serve as rationalities for the evaluation of standards and data quality, but also for the link between data production, distribution and analysis on one side and specific common goods on the other side. Different data worlds can be identified as ideal types, which are characterized by different combinations of these orders of worth and quality conventions. In Western countries, these data worlds coexist and can be conceived of as different institutional rationalities, which are the blueprints for real organizational settings. The data worlds of official statistics, of academic science, of the civic data worlds are the most visible ones. Another data world is the big data world, whose algorithms and practices of data analysis are mainly invisible. This set of mentioned data worlds does not claim to be a complete one, but it has been useful so far to serve for contributions to a sociology of social research.[4] And these worlds are in transition for different reasons. One reason is the tension between them, because in many situations these actors from some of these data worlds criticize practices, standards and effects of other data worlds. Another reason is that these data worlds cannot rely equally on data generating infrastructures, such as Internet platforms, and are influenced in different ways by new technologies, such as artificial intelligence and intense development and usage of algorithms. Some of these data worlds can be briefly sketched.

The oldest data world is the *academic science data* world, which can be clearly identified with universities and research institutes. Here, the industrial convention and the convention of inspiration are most influential. The academic data world aims to generate new methods and knowledge to improve technologies (most visibly with engineering and computer sciences) as well to advance mankind. This data world influenced the following ones, but still sticks to its claim to be impartial and not to legitimize itself with economic or public engagements. The data world of *official statistics* emerged in the course of the last one and a half centuries. It co-emerged with industrialization and the development of statist bureaucracy. Official statistics is in most countries based on specific law, which equipped the institutions of official statistics with a high degree of legitimacy and power. Official statistics data worlds can rely on public administration as data generating and data sorting infrastructure. It delivers data reports and publishes indicators with a long-term orientation and with a high degree of visibility.

The official statistics world is mainly structured by the industrial and the civic conventions and has long aimed to support but also to legitimate state policies. In its beginnings, official statistics was oriented mainly toward state administrations but it reoriented more and more toward national and international publics. One reason for this was the critique of the civic society, which claimed for a more public service orientation of official statistics. The *civic data world* can be conceived as emerging from social movements, non-governmental organizations (NGOs) and other civic actors and civic agencies, which collect and generate data to report on social issues and to build up empirical evidence for their claims. The civic data world is mainly influenced by combinations of the civic convention, the industrial convention, the domestic convention and the network convention. This world aims to engage for civilian's participation and its identity is based essentially on forging a countervailing power against private and administrative forms of governance as well as to build up agency and critical capacities on data and data transparency. A more recent form of engagement is data activism, wherein scientists and civic actors cooperate to detect unfair and illegitimate forms of data-based governance, identify unintended and irrational consequences of software and algorithms and work on the application of algorithms to support civilian engagements (Milan and van der Velden, 2016; Didier, 2018).[5] Also, organizations in this civic data world try to critically scrutinize algorithms applied to civilians and public issues and claim for transparency and public deliberation of algorithms.[6] Initiatives such as "open source", "open data", "open science" (Kitchin, 2014; Baack, 2015) or "citizen science" (Franzosi and Sauermann, 2014; Kitchin, 2014) can be regarded as part of this data world as well as engagements to build up more flexible and more adequate data infrastructures to generate data, which is useful for public agency (Lane, 2020a, 2020b).

The *big data world* is in some important respects different from the official statistics data world and the civic data world, because it exploits the privatized access and control of big data generating infrastructures as Internet platforms and data markets. Also, data analysis is run by intensely applying advanced techniques such as developing new algorithms and applying machine learning techniques and artificial intelligence (Mayer-Schönberger and Cukier, 2013). Another characteristic is that its techniques, algorithms and data analytics are not only handled as private companies' assets, but these devices are also opaque and invisible to the public. Although companies from the big data world (most notably Google) provide free services to the public, this data world is criticized by the civic data world for the opacity of its algorithms and the privatization of its huge amounts of data. It is an open (and contested) question whether the big data world does aim for a common good. Evidently, the companies aim for profit in this data world. Even if all data worlds have to apply algorithms (e.g., in statistical data analysis software), it is the big data world which is criticized for aiming to analyze and to influence individuals' behavior (Zuboff, 2019).

Nowadays, one can find new alliances between these sketched worlds and also combinations. For example, more and more state departments apply advanced algorithms and big data analytics to detect criminal behavior or to survey their citizens. But it is also state departments which align with civic agencies and NGOs to enhance public capacities to understand algorithms, their effects of public life and to advance public concerns.[7] Actors from the civic data world, the academic science data world and the official big data world try to form coalitions to implement new data infrastructures as alternatives to the privately owned Internet platforms (Kitchin, 2014; Owen-Smith, 2018; Lane, 2020a, 2020b).

Analyzing Algorithmic Regulations: Critique in Situations of Uncertainty

The totality of rules and regulations to which people are exposed in digital contexts can be explained by the dynamics of conventions, rights and normative systems. As has been shown, these norms are partly visible, but partly hidden in technical contexts. The entanglement of different areas of society in which norms are set and in which shifts in norm-setting occur has led to a complex structure of regulators that is quite difficult to grasp at times. Formal law is set by states, digital platforms are regulated in their terms and conditions and normative ideas are inscribed in codes and algorithms. Especially in recent years, the debate around these issues has led to a number of regulatory projects, transparency efforts and clarification of responsibilities.

To understand how actors try to cope with *black boxes*, different normative approaches and new technologies, it is critical to distinguish between different coordinative goals and ideas of the public good. Thẹse are factors that come to play amongst different actors in – and coalitions between – data worlds during efforts of reshaping data structures and establishing transparency and accountabilities in a world that seems to be dominated by logics of commercial big data companies and their opaque deployment of algorithms.

A key to understanding the critical capacities (Boltanski and Thévenot, 1999) of such actors and therefore the encounter of normative and justificatory differences is the situational visibility of algorithmic decision-making (ADM) processes, be it in situations of content moderation on platforms or algorithmic decisions in public administrations. Whenever an actor is noticeably affected by such a decision, situations of uncertainty and critique may be observable.

Taking the examples of content moderation and other surfacing ADM processes as an observable and therefore criticizable[8] part of algorithmic regulation, the described logics of data worlds and the EC/SC approach allow for casting light on the complex dynamics of algorithmic regulation and help reveal functionalities, necessities and justifications amongst the involved actors.

The emergence and the power of the big data world and the economically driven large-scale usage of data in commercial contexts made private companies establish ADM processes as a *conditio sine qua non.*[9] Especially digital content-platforms brought the use of big data to perfection. Self-conceptualized as neutral places where people meet and interact, large amounts of individual and general data were collected and analyzed to improve both user experiences and advertisement. Here, the opacity of algorithms is very high, and users usually won't be aware of sorting algorithms, the categorizations and quantifications that strongly shape their experience online.

Established and approved in micro targeting, advertising services and categorization, ADM also appeared to be the perfect choice when interventions on content and users were no longer viable (Gillespie, 2020). Broadly labeled as *content moderation*, all interventions toward media, text or observable interactions of users have in common that they constitute direct and at least partially visible interventions on users and their actions online (Gillespie, 2020; Gorwa et al., 2020).

Even though there have always been intrinsic motivations for companies not to have certain content[10] on their platforms, when it later came to questions of copyright (Perel and Elkin-Koren, 2016: 484) or speech restrictions (Heldt, 2019: 3–4), the urge to moderate content on a larger scale came – generally speaking – mostly from external pressure by governments and the civil society. Platforms found themselves in a tension between different ideas of public good that were brought to them externally. Together with their very own ideas of restricting certain content, a complex environment of moderating and regulating regimes was established on most of the large platforms for user-generated content such as Facebook, Twitter, YouTube or Instagram (Gorwa et al., 2020: 6) but also in search engines and intermediaries like payment service providers (Tusikov, 2017: 22–25).

> That platforms operate their moderation practices under a complex web of nebulous rules and procedural opacity renders situations […] even more challenging, with governments and others clamoring for tighter controls on some material, and other members of civil society demanding greater freedoms for online expression […].
>
> (Roberts, 2018)

The problematic notions of online content moderation are just one of several examples, where ADM processes (with their hidden values and normativities) are directly interwoven with concrete ideas of norms and norm enforcement. When it comes to governmental decisions, as in public administration or organizational procedures like human resource management, the use of big data approaches offers easy, scalable and reliable solutions but remains linked to the problems of opaque norms, values and measurements within automations.

Such situations where actors are notably affected by algorithmic decisions could generally be grasped as *situations of uncertainty* for different actors. Herein, a plurality of requirements and logics of regulation, measurement conventions and automation culminates in situations where algorithms may still operate opaquely but not unseen in their outcomes. On an individual level, human attention might first and foremost be paid by the moderated user, whose tweet, YouTube video or Facebook post was blocked, deleted or labeled as problematic (Myers West, 2018), by a citizen who was denied a public service (Allhutter et al., 2020) or an employee who was dismissed (Soper, 2021). On a larger scale, the outcomes of content moderation or other problematic automated decisions are situationally structured as well (Barthe et al., 2013: IV) and may come to the attention of platform operators, government officials or NGOs. It is important to mention that the neopragmatist notion of situation does not only cover configurations occurring in simultaneous moments and places, but also distributed, stretched and interrupted constellations in which actors coordinate their actions (Diaz-Bone, 2011: 49).

EC/SC has mobilized situations of uncertainty as observation points, where actors are confronted with situations that require a conscious decision, which must be justified with a reference to a specific kind of common good usually linked to conventions. As such situations of norm enforcement do not only affect actors of the big data world but also single users, the state and the civil society, other justifications than those from the mere big data logic, must be brought up. This causes an epistemological breaking point that could be utilized as a potential bottle opener for some of the opaque logics that are hidden within algorithmic *black boxes*. As such situations however won't be able to explain the hidden norm-based quantifications and classifications within ADM processes entirely, they offer a leverage point to force engaged actors to justify their actions.

As big data has brought the usage of algorithmic regulation and automated decision-making to a standard in regulating, moderating and sorting large amounts of data, the promises of *objective, fair* and *reliable* data-based decisions convinced not only commercial actors but also governments. With their history in official statistics (Desrosières, 2009, 2011) and an interest in both enforcement and efficiency (Engstrom et al., 2020: 22), governmental actors are principally open to the employment of similar approaches of decision-making, often directly offered by private companies (Engstrom et al, 2020: 7). Mainly structured by the industrial convention and the civic convention, the market convention (as in the big data world) is less applicable in bureaucratic situations. Nevertheless, problems of training data quality, incoherencies and classificational errors persist. Such problems may be marginalized and less problematized in commercial contexts but are of greater importance and target of *critique* within legally defined boundaries of public administration. States are usually subjected to greater demands and duties for transparency and accountability than private firms. Also, these transparencies enable actors from the civil society to criticize and intervene in state-driven projects.

Actors from the civic data world have not yet distinguished themselves through the extensive use of ADM processes on their own, but their expertise and their common good-related goals such as freedom, nondiscrimination and equality are important when it comes to initiating criticizable situations on a large scale. NGOs collect single-case reports and workout reports, e.g., on structural discrimination, biases and in transparencies, both in private and public application areas.

Meanwhile, an important source of justification for such critique often comes from a data world that is at the same time involved in developing the technical foundations and, because of its profound knowledge, is also aware of their limitations and problems. Unlike the big data world, the academic science data world is strongly interested in epistemological knowledge and less in the (commercial) usability of knowledge. Trained in theories and philosophy of science, the implication of falsifications and epistemology, academic data scientists are an important source of critique when it comes to tackling the very base of big data (Kitchin, 2014, 2017; Symons and Alvarado, 2016), promoting the idea of critical data studies in science (Iliadis and Russo, 2016) and education (Pangrazio and Selwyn, 2021) or even pointing out the linkage between norms and measurements (Desrosières, 2008, 2014; Diaz-Bone 2016, 2017, 2019; Diaz-Bone and Didier, 2016; Diaz-Bone and Horvath, 2021). Despite a greater access to and understanding of the structure of algorithms (Zweig et al., 2018; Krafft et al., 2021), this kind of academic critique also relies on *situations of uncertainty*, even though they are intentionally brought to light by researchers to challenge platforms and governments:

> To hold software service and platform providers accountable, it is necessary to create trustworthy, quantified evidence of problematic algorithmic decisions, e.g., by large-scale black box analyses.
> (Krafft et al., 2021: 143)

When it comes to algorithmic regulation, data worlds are entangled in a complex constellation of reciprocal critique and sometimes find themselves in processes of norm setting or duties to enforce norms – depending on their different capabilities to regulate. But how does critique in situations of uncertainty shape actual regulatory regimes and how do actors coordinate and justify their actions in this regard? The next section will bring this issue to life by examining selected empirical phenomena in which ADM processes are applied.

New Regulators – New Perspectives on Regulatory Processes

While successfully pursuing goals of data-driven business such as surveillance, ad targeting and general data collection, big data actors found themselves as regulators on their own and de facto enforcers of legal and other external norms. Using often opaque and therefore hardly criticizable automation, several areas of the digitalizing society are affected by new and not thoroughly overviewable regulatory processes. There is more than just a duality of regulators – state and big data actors – who determine the regulatory environments that users, citizens, employees or customers are confronted with in digital everyday life. It is the complex interplay between data worlds and those who act and react within them who justify, criticize, evaluate and develop not just technically but more importantly convention-based. Situations of uncertainty provide a leverage point to observe such action, coordination and critique.

The proposed scheme to analyze new regulatory areas and processes by mobilizing the critical capacities of actors within data worlds and the conventions they rely on promises worthy insights into several areas of algorithmic regulation. The following five are a cursory account of some of them, with suggestions which situations of uncertainty do or may come up and how critique is made possible and justified by ideas of common goods. This should provide an overview of how broad and widespread both the usage of ADM processes and the potential of its convention-based analysis are.

1   *Big-data platforms and the enforcement of copyright and speech regulations* are the most notable examples when it comes to the large-scale enforcement of legal norms by online service providers. Uncertainty may occur for users who post or upload disputably (il)legal content. At the same time, there is uncertainty (e.g., for rights holders) on whether they get royalties for copyrighted materials (Leistner and Metzger, 2017) or for those who are addressed by disputably offensive speech (Heldt, 2019). As the big data world tended to justify their automated moderation decisions on copyright and hate speech (Gorwa et al., 2020: 6) from an industrial convention, critique is mainly fueled by civic data world actors, e.g., NGOs, but also the scientific data world come from a civic and domestic convention. As algorithms are currently said to come to their limits in borderline cases (Elkin-Koren, 2017), such as sampling, quotes or satirist or pastiche content, state regulators, e.g., in Europe, started to force platforms to install ex post of human-based out-of-court resolutions (European Commission, 2020; Cauffman and Goanta, 2021: 12–13; Quintais and Schwemer, 2021: 16) and ex ante possibilities to pre-flag, e.g., fair-use content (Metzger and Senftleben, 2020: 128). This could be grasped as an endeavor to enable transparency for outcomes of algorithmic decisions and to enable and inform users to act in such uncertain situations. At the same time, in a similar ex post fashion, Facebook

installed its own widely discussed (Douek, 2019; Klonick, 2019; Golia, 2021) *oversight board* to criticize, evaluate and oversee its own actions in an alleged independent manner. Such an action acknowledges the need for insights, critique and control, but does, as critics put it, not adequately answer questions on independent control.

2   The vast amounts of regulatory power do also come with their own uncertainties as *big data platforms and enforcement regarding child sexual abuse imagery and terroristic content* illustrate. As there is no dispute on the common good of not wanting to have such content available, questions of the borders' enforcement and surveillance come up and must be justified. After successfully developing and implementing automated recognition systems for abuse imagery such as *PhotoDNA* (Farid, 2018) or terrorist content such as the *Shared Industry Hash Database* (Gorwa et al., 2020: 2), there may be uncertainties and need for justifications for online service providers where to technically stop surveilling and how to handle different qualities of nonbinding requests from governmental officials, binding court decisions (Fisherman, 2019: 90) and soft requests from the civic society (Bursztein et al., 2019: 1). Such delicate topics are also a source of uncertainty for civic actors as NGOs who criticize surveillance but agree with the goal of removing abuse imagery and terrorist material (Perez, 2014).

3   While the cases mentioned above have their restrictions legally defined, there are socio-normative conflicts within the big data world, e.g., *ethically driven disputes between porn platforms and payment services* where platforms regulate in different but highly impactful ways that are partially dispatched from legal questions. The repeatedly surfacing conflict (Tusikov, 2021: 73–74) between payment service providers such as PayPal, Visa or Mastercard and porn platforms, most notably Pornhub, revolving around the accessibility of payment options for users and actors and vice versa the availability of user-uploaded, unverified content. Incidents such as the suspension of payments or the instant deletion of over ten million nonofficial videos by Pornhub in 2020 (Kastrenakes, 2020) showcase the enormous regulatory power such platforms have, especially in grey areas of society (Tusikov, 2021: 75–76). This conflict is coined by reciprocal uncertainty whether it is ethically justifiable to offer payments for adult content or whether pornography business models for both actors and platforms could prevail.

4   As examples 1–3 illustrate the potential of big data actors as important regulators and enforcing actors, another impactful and critical application field of ADM is *public administration and the usage of big data technologies*. As mentioned, public administrations that are connected to the world of official statistics and therefore classifications of citizens are structurally open for the application of big data-driven sorting and decision-supporting algorithms that either directly stem from private big data companies (who often exclusively have the data required to offer certain services) or are developed under comparable premises and conventions. While administrative acts underlie more explicit public accountabilities and formal law, ADM systems are more and more in use by state agencies (Engstrom et al., 2020). Critical questions in regard to accountability and explainability are crucial in democratically controlled administrative processes:

> When public officials deny benefits or make decisions affecting the public's rights, the law generally requires them to explain why.
>
> (Engstrom et al., 2020: 7)

The hurdles for an implementation of such technologies appear higher, which is mainly due to the strong civic convention and the common good of a nondiscriminatory and transparent democracy. In such cases, formal law simultaneously functions as a coordinative framework and a guardrail for those who implement. That critique from external actors from the academic or the civic data world remains crucial, is shown by several cases, e.g., where authorities have used prediction algorithms in Austrian job centers (Allhutter et al., 2020), language recognition programs in German asylum processes (Keiner, 2020) or privately run person-based technologies in predictive policing in Canada (Robertson et al., 2020: 47–50) that sparked public critique and controversy and forced actors to justify their actions. Situations of uncertainty come up amongst those who are affected by such decisions, e.g., when assessments are wrong or predictions are discriminatory or biased. In the course of public outcry, uncertainty emerges for public administrators who have to justify the use of such technologies without (sometimes) being fully capable of seeing through the opaque interior of both databases and algorithms.

5   The last of the five application areas is at the very intersection between commercial, formally legal and civic logics and an interesting outlook on further challenges of ADM. Legal tech is an

intersection between big data and legal norms. Legal tech describes the application of big data technologies on legal services. Even though the large-scale use of legal tech is still in its early stages, here different dynamics are observable than in the other areas mentioned above. As legal tech is *per definitionem* strongly interwoven with legal norms, there is no notion of ex post interference of law with existing business models as in the mere big data world, but law itself becomes a target of applying such logics. Turned this way, law and big data ADM seem to be made for each other. Both appear to rely on a logical, structural framework where step-by-step transformations from data into outputs are made (Pasquale, 2019: 1). Since the beginnings of computer technologies, law has been subject to (usually academic or political) endeavors of cybernetics and digitization (Salami, 2017). With commercial approaches and ADM technologies, the digitization of only seemingly simple legal processes such as legal forms, contract generation or contesting speeding tickets (Pasquale, 2019: 12–18; Hähnchen et al., 2020: 631) started to become a business model.

The big data world again promises efficient, precise and scalable automations that find fruitful soil amongst commercial branches of legal administration such as law firms and lawyers (Hartung et al., 2018). Academic scholars discussing the potential of legal automation use their insights in both legal and computational processes to confront big data promises with critique from civic and domestic conventions that point out not just misconceptions of the formal logics of legal syllogisms (Pasquale, 2019; Hähnchen et al., 2020) but general uncertainties for legal professionals, clients and plaintiffs who may face typical imprecisions, opacities, simplifications or even biases that come with ADM (Engstrom and Gelbach, 2020: 1024). The common good of due process and the specially protected attorney-client relationship could hardly be upheld when big data scalability and automation are central coordinative goals (Pasquale, 2019: 60).

With these five exemplary fields of application in mind, EC/SC's perspective view on regulatory configurations and their situational settings casts a light on the intertwining of state and private regulation, as both of them are more and more enforced by ADM processes and therefore dominated by big data logics and their inherent conventions. While those processes come with contested yet often convincing promises of objectivity, efficiency and scalability, their opacities and lacking accountabilities become an emerging problem for otherwise well-established controlling mechanisms.

Critique and reciprocal justifications, brought up by directly involved actors or actors capable of overseeing larger contexts, depend on information and clarification. The approach of utilizing situations of uncertainty to formulate critique and demand justifications helps to identify not only existing conflict points but shows strikingly how necessary it is to have constant accountabilities not just in a legal but also a social manner. As unsolved problems with biases, discrimination, erroneous decisions and the blending of commercial and common good goals show, the important mechanisms of critique and justification are weakened when observability is either impossible or optional and only occasionally admitted.

Notes

1 Technically seen, an algorithm is a finite set of calculative steps, which are organized in an ordered sequence (that allows a selection of steps and/ or loops) and which transforms a data input in an output. An algorithm is realized as a code sequence in a programming language, i.e., software (Louridas, 2020: 19/23/26).
2 The term "algorithmic governance" was introduced by Müller-Birn et al. (2013); see, for a sketch of this notion and its genealogy, Katzenbach and Ulbricht (2019).
3 As O'Neil therefore has stated, algorithms can be conceived as "an opinion formalized in code" (O'Neil, 2016: 49).
4 See for more details Diaz-Bone et al. (2020) and Diaz-Bone and Horvath (2021).
5 See, e.g., the movement of "Statactivisme" in France (Bruno et al., 2014; Didier, 2018), "MyData" in Finland (Lehtiniemi and Ruckenstein, 2019) or "DataKind" in the USA.
6 One example is "Algorithm Watch", see https://algorithmwatch.org/en/
7 One example in Germany is Civic Coding, see https://www.civic-coding.de/
8 In the sense of critics by enlightened actors as Boltanski (2011) describes it.
9 Even mass-scale human decisions as in *click working content moderation* is deeply embedded in preceding algorithmic or AI sorting and deciding what is to be displayed to the human moderators. For Facebook, see, e.g., Vincent (2020).
10 Such as pornography, violent content or spam.

References

Allhutter, D., Cech, F., Fischer, F., Grill, G., and Mager, A. (2020). Algorithmic profiling of job seekers in Austria: How austerity politics are made effective. *Frontiers in Big Data*, 3(5). https://doi.org/10.3389/fdata.2020.00005
Baack, S. (2015). Datafication and empowerment: How the open data movement re-articulates notions of democracy, participation, and journalism. *Big Data and Society*, 2(2), 1–11. https://doi.org/10.1177/2053951715594634

Barthe, Y., de Blic, D., Heurtin, J., Lagneau, É., Lemieux, C., Linhardt, D., and Trom, D. (2013). Pragmatic sociology: A user's guide. *Politix*, 103, I-XXVI. https://doi.org/10.3917/pox.103.0175

Beer, D. (2016). *Metric power.* Palgrave Macmillan.

Beer, D. (2017). The social power of algorithms. *Information, Communication & Society*, 20(1), 1–13. https://doi.org/10.1080/1369118X.2016.1216147

Boltanski, L. (2011). *On critique: A sociology of emancipation.* Polity Press.

Boltanski, L., and Thévenot, L. (1999). The sociology of critical capacity. *European Journal of Social Theory*, 2(3), 359–377. https://doi.org/10.1177%2F136843199002003010

Boltanski, L., and Thévenot, L. (2006). *On justification. Economies of worth.* Princeton University Press.

Botsman, R. (2017, October 21). *Big data meets big brother as China moves to rate its citizens.* Wired. https://www.wired.co.uk/article/chinese-government-social-credit-score-privacy-invasion

Bruno, I., Didier, E., and Prévieux J. (2014). *Statactivisme. Comment lutter avec des nombres.* La Découverte.

Burrell, J., and Fourcade, M. (2021). The society of algorithms. *Annual Review of Sociology*, 47, 1–23. https://doi.org/10.1146/annurev-soc-090820-020800

Bursztein, E., Clarke, E., DeLaune, M., Elifff, D.M., Hsu, N., Olson, L., Shehan, J., Thakur, M., Thomas, K., and Bright, T. (2019). Rethinking the detection of child sexual abuse imagery on the Internet. In The World Wide Web Conference (WWW '19). *Association for Computing Machinery*, 2601–2607. https://doi.org/10.1145/3308558.3313482

Cauffman, C., and Goanta, C. (2021). A new order: The digital services act and consumer protection. *European Journal of Risk Regulation*, 1–17. https://doi.org/10.1017/err.2021.8

Centemeri, L. (2012). The contribution of the sociology of quantification to a discussion of objectivity economics. In J. Castro Caldas and V. Neves (Eds.), *Facts, values and objectivity in economics* (pp. 110–125). Routledge.

Desrosières, A. (2000). Measurement and its uses: Harmonization and quality in social statistics. *International Statistical Review*, 68(2), 173–187. https://doi.org/10.1111/j.1751-5823.2000.tb00320.x

Desrosières, A. (2008). Pour une sociologie historique de la quantification. *MinesTech.*

Desrosières, A. (2009). How to be real and conventional: A discussion of the quality criteria of official statistics. *Minerva*, 47, 307–322. https://doi.org/10.1007/s11024-009-9125-3

Desrosières, A. (2011). Words and numbers. For a sociology of the statistical argument. In A. Saetnan, H. Lomell and S. Hammer (Eds.), *The mutual construction of statistics and society* (pp. 41–63). Routledge.

Desrosières, A. (2014). *Prouver et gouverner. Une analyse politique des statistiques publiques.* La Découverte.

Desrosières, A. (2015). Retroaction: How indicators feed back onto quantified actors. In R. Rottenburg, S. E. Merry, S. J. Park and J. Mugler (Eds.), *The world of indicators. The making of governmental knowledge through quantification* (pp. 329–353). Cambridge University Press.

Diaz-Bone, R. (2011). The methodological standpoint of the "économie des conventions". *Historical Social Research*, 36(4), 43–63. https://doi.org/10.12759/hsr.36.2011.4.43-63

Diaz-Bone, R. (2016). Convention theory, classification and quantification. *Historical Social Research*, 41(2), 48–71. https://doi.org/10.12759/hsr.41.2016.2.48-71

Diaz-Bone, R. (2017). Classifications, quantifications and quality conventions in markets – Perspectives of the economics of convention. *Historical Social Research*, 42(1), 238–262. https://doi.org/10.12759/hsr.42.2017.1.238-262

Diaz-Bone, R. (2018). *Die "Economie des conventions". Grundlagen und Entwicklungen der neuen französischen Wirtschaftssoziologie* (2nd ed.). Springer VS.

Diaz-Bone, R. (2019). Statistical panopticism and its critique. *Historical Social Research*, 44(2), 77–102. https://doi.org/10.12759/hsr.44.2019.2.77-102

Diaz-Bone, R., and Didier, E. (Eds.). (2016). Conventions and quantification – Transdisciplinary perspectives on statistics and classifications (special issue). *Historical Social Research*, 41(2).

Diaz-Bone, R., and Horvath, K. (2021). Official statistics, big data and civil society. Introducing the approach of "economics of convention" for understanding the rise of new data worlds and their im-plications. *Statistical Journal of the International Organization of Official Statistics*, 37(2021), 219–228. http://doi.org/10.3233/SJI-200733

Diaz-Bone, R., and Salais, R. (Eds.). (2011). Conventions and institutions from a historical perspective (special issue). *Historical Social Research*, 36(4).

Diaz-Bone, R., Horvath, K., and Cappel, V. (2020). Social research in times of big data. The challenges of new data worlds and the need for a sociology of social research. *Historical Social Research*, 45(3), 314–341. https://doi.org/10.12759/hsr.45.2020.3.314-341.

Didier, E. (2018). Globalization of quantitative policing: Between management and statactivism. *Annual Review of Sociology* 44, 515–534. https://doi.org/10.1146/annurev-soc-060116-053308

Douek, E. (2019). Facebook's oversight board: Move fast with stable infrastructure and humility. *NCJL & Tech*, 21, 1–77.

Dourish, P. (2016). Algorithms and their others. Algorithmic culture in context. *Big Data and Society*, 3(1), 1–11. https://doi.org/10.1177%2F2053951716665128

Elkin-Koren, N. (2017). Fair use by design. *UCLA Law Review*, 64, 1082–1100.

Engstrom, D. F., and Gelbach, J. B. (2020). Legal tech, civil procedure, and the future of adversarialism. *University of Pennsylvania Law Review*, 169, 1001–1099.

Engstrom, D. F., Ho, D. E., Sharkey, C. M., and Cuéllar, M. (2020). Government by algorithm: Artificial intelligence in federal administrative agencies. *NYU School of Law, Public Law Research Paper*, No. 20–54. http://dx.doi.org/10.2139/ssrn.3551505

Eubanks, V. (2017). *Automating inequality. How high-tech tools profile, police, and punish the poor.* St. Martin's Press.

European Commission. (2020). *The Digital Services Act: Ensuring a safe and accountable online environment*. European Commission. https://ec.europa.eu/info/strategy/priorities-2019-2024/europe-fit-digital-age/digital-services-act-ensuring-safe-and-accountable-online-environment_en

Eymard-Duvernay, F. (Ed.). (2006a). *L'économie des conventions. Méthodes et résultats. Vol. 1: Débats*. La Découverte.

Eymard-Duvernay, F. (Ed.). (2006b). *L'économie des conventions. Méthodes et résultats. Vol. 2: Développements*. La Découverte.

Farid, H. (2018). Reining in online abuses. *Technology and Innovation*, 19, 593–599. https://doi.org/10.21300/19.3.2018.593

Fisherman, B. (2019). Crossroads: Counter-Terrorism and the Internet. *Texas National Security Review*, 2(2), 83–100. https://doi.org/10.26153/tsw/1942

Fourcade, M., and Healy, K. (2013). Classification situations: Life-chances in the neoliberal era. *Accounting, Organizations and Society*, 38(8), 559–572. http://dx.doi.org/10.1016/j.aos.2013.11.002

Gillespie, T. (2020). Content moderation, AI, and the question of scale. *Big Data and Society*, 7(2), 1–5. https://doi.org/10.1177/2053951720943234

Golia, A. (2021). Beyond oversight: Advancing societal constitutionalism in the age of surveillance capitalism. http://dx.doi.org/10.2139/ssrn.3793219

Gorwa, R., Binns, R., and Katzenbach, C. (2020). Algorithmic content moderation: Technical and political challenges in the automation of platform governance. *Big Data and Society*, 7(1), 1–15. https://doi.org/10.1177/2053951719897945

Hähnchen, S., Schrader, P. T., Weller, F., and Wischmeyer, T. (2020). Rechtsanwendung durch Menschen als Auslaufmodell? *Juristische Schulung*, 7, 626–635.

Hartung, M., Bues, M. M., and Halbleib, G. (Eds.). (2018). *Legal tech. How technology is changing the legal world. A practitioner's guide*. Beck.

Heldt, A. (2019). Reading between the lines and the numbers: an analysis of the first NetzDG reports. *Internet Policy Review*, 8(2). http://doi.org/10.14763/2019.2.1398

Iliadis, A., and Russo, F. (2016). Critical data studies: An introduction. *Big Data and Society*, 3(2) 1–7. https://doi.org/10.1177/2053951716674238

Kastrenakes, J. (2020, December 14). *Pornhub just removed most of its videos*. The Verge. https://www.theverge.com/2020/12/14/22173858/pornhub-videos-removed-user-uploaded-visa-mastercard-verified

Katzenbach, C., and Ulbricht, L. (2019). Algorithmic governance. *Internet Policy Review*, 8(4). https://doi.org/10.14763/2019.4.1424

Keiner, A. (2020). Algorithmen als Rationalitätsmythos. Fernuniversität Hagen. http://dx.doi.org/10.18445/20200727-094744-0

Kitchin, R. (2014). The data revolution. *Big data, open data, data infrastructures and their consequences*. Sage.

Kitchin, R. (2017). Thinking critically about and research algorithms. *Information, Communication and Society*, 20(1), 14–29. https://doi.org/10.1080/1369118X.2016.1154087

Klonick, K. (2019). The Facebook Oversight Board: Creating an independent institution to adjudicate online free expression. *Yale Law Journal*, 129, 2418–2499.

Krafft, T. D., Reber, M., Krafft, R., Coutrier, A., and Zweig, K. A. (2021). Crucial challenges in large-scale black box analyses. In L. Boratto, S. Faralli, M. Marras, and G. Stilo (Eds.), *Advances in bias and fairness in information retrieval. BIAS 2021. Communications in computer and information science* (Vol. 1418, pp. 143–155). Springer. https://doi.org/10.1007/978-3-030-78818-6_13

Lane, J. (2020a). After Covid-19, the US statistical system needs to change. *Significance*, (4), 42–43. https://doi.org/10.1111/1740-9713.01428

Lane, J. (2020b). *Democratizing our data*. MIT Press.

Lash, S. (2007). Power after hegemony. Cultural studies in mutation? *Theory, Culture and Society*, 24(3), 55–78. https://doi.org/10.1177%2F0263276407075956

Lazer, D., and Radford, J. (2017). Data ex machina. Introduction to Big Data. *Annual Review of Sociology*, 43, 19–39. https://doi.org/10.1146/annurev-soc-060116-053457

Lehtiniemi, T., and Ruckenstein, M. (2019). The social imaginaries of data activism. *Big Data and Society*, 6(1), 1–12. https://doi.org/10.1177%2F2053951718821146

Leistner, M., and Metzger, A. (2017). The EU Copyright package: A way out of the dilemma in two stages. *International Review of Intellectual Property and Competition*, 48, 381–384. https://doi.org/10.1007/s40319-017-0586-x

Louridas, P. (2020). *Algorithms*. MIT Press.

Mayer-Schönberger, V., and Cukier, K. (2013). *Big data. A revolution that will transform how we live, work, and think*. John Murray Publishers.

Mayer-Schönberger, V., and Ramge, T. (2018). *Reinventing capitalism in the age of big data*. Basic Books.

Mejias, U. A., and Couldry, N. (2019). Datafication. *Internet Policy Review*, 8(4). https://doi.org/10.14763/2019.4.1428

Metzger, A., and Senftleben, M. (2020). Selected aspects of implementing Article 17 of the directive on Copyright in the digital single market into national law – Comment of the European Copyright Society. *JIPITEC*, 11, 115–131.

Milan, S., and van der Velden, L. (2016). The alternative epistemologies of data activism. *Digital Culture and Society*, 2(2), 57–74. https://doi.org/10.14361/dcs-2016-0205

Müller-Birn, C., Herbsleb, J., and Dobusch, L. (2013). Work-to-rule: The emergence of algorithmic governance in Wikipedia. *Proceedings of the 6th International Conference on Communities and Technologies*, 80–89. https://doi.org/10.1145/2482991.2482999

Myers West, S. (2018). Censored, suspended, shadowbanned: User interpretations of content moderation on social media platforms. *New Media & Society*, 20(11), 4366–4383. https://doi.org/10.1177/1461444818773059

O'Neil, C. (2016). *Weapons of math destruction. How big data in-creases inequality and threatens democracy.* Crown Publishers.

Owen-Smith, J. (2018). *Research universities and the public good. Discovery for an uncertain future.* Stanford University Press.

Pangrazio, L., and Selwyn, N. (2021). Towards a school-based 'critical data education'. *Pedagogy, Culture & Society*, 29(3), 431–448. https://doi.org/10.1080/14681366.2020.1747527

Pasquale, F. (2015). *The black box society. The secret algorithms that control money and information.* Harvard University Press.

Pasquale, F. (2019). A rule of persons, not machines: The limits of legal automation. *George Washington Law Review*, 87(1), 1–60.

Peeters, R., and Schuilenburg, M. (2021). The algorithmic society. An introduction. In M. Schuilenburg, and R. Peeters (Eds.), *The algorithmic society. Technology, Power, and Knowledge* (pp. 1–16). Routledge.

Perel, M., and Elkin-Koren, N. (2016). Accountability in algorithmic Copyright enforcement. *Stanford Technology Law Review*, 473–533. https://dx.doi.org/10.2139/ssrn.2607910

Perez, S. (2014, August 6). Why the gmail scan that led to a man's arrest for child porn was not a privacy violation. *TechCrunch*. http://tcrn.ch/XEMKnA

Quintais, J., and Schwemer, S. F. (2021). The interplay between the digital services act and sector regulation: How special is copyright? http://dx.doi.org/10.2139/ssrn.3841606

Roberts, S. T. (2018). Digital detritus: 'Error' and the logic of opacity in social media content moderation. *First Monday*, 23(3). https://doi.org/10.5210/fm.v23i3.8283

Robertson, K., Khoo, C., and Song, Y. (2020). *To surveil and predict. A human rights analysis of algorithmic policing in Canada.* University of Toronto.

Salami, E. (2017). A brief overview of legal informatics. http://dx.doi.org/10.2139/ssrn.2966201

Soper, S. (2021, June 28). *Fired by Bot at Amazon: 'It's you against the machine'.* Bloomberg. https://www.bloomberg.com/news/features/2021-06-28/fired-by-bot-amazon-turns-to-machine-managers-and-workers-are-losing-out

Steiner, C. (2012). *Automate this. How algorithms came to rule our world.* Penguin.

Storper, M., and Salais, R. (1997). *Worlds of production. The action frameworks of the economy.* Harvard University Press.

Symons, J., and Alvarado, R. (2016). Can we trust Big Data? Applying philosophy of science to software. *Big Data and Society*, 3(2), 1–17. https://doi.org/10.1177/2053951716664747

The Economist. (2016, December 17). *China's digital dictatorship – Big Data and government.* The Economist. https://www.economist.com/leaders/2016/12/17/chinas-digital-dictatorship

Tusikov, N. (2017). *Chokepoints: Global private regulation on the Internet.* University of California Press.

Tusikov, N. (2021). Censoring sex: Payment platforms' regulation of sexual expression. In M. Deflem and D. M. D. Silva (Eds.), *Media and law: Between free speech and censorship* (Sociology of Crime, Law and Deviance, Vol. 26, (pp. 63–79). Emerald Publishing.

Vincent, J. (2020, November 13). *Facebook is now using AI to sort content for quicker moderation.* The Verge. https://www.theverge.com/2020/11/13/21562596/facebook-ai-moderation

Zuboff, S. (2019). *The age of surveillance capitalism. The fight for a human future at the new frontier of power.* Public Affairs.

Zweig, K. A., Wenzelburger, G., and Krafft, T. D. (2018). On chances and risks of security related algorithmic decision making systems. *European Journal for Security Research*, 3, 181–203. https://doi.org/10.1007/s41125-018-0031-2

3 From Big to Democratic Data

Why the Rise of AI Needs Data Solidarity

Mercedes Bunz and Photini Vrikki

Digital technologies and their processing of data have transformed our cultural, social and working lives through expansive digital connections and networks, allowing us to undertake social, cultural and economic transactions that shape global and local communities. This digital space is a sphere in which users interact, thereby creating data, which is then collected and analyzed shaping their societal possibilities through recommendations or algorithmic decision-making. Yet, paradoxically, in spite of the ubiquitous reach of our digital condition, the *political force* within data shaping our societies is only in parts understood. One reason for this is that the notion of "big data" at the beginning of the 21st century has been conceptualized *by* businesses and *for* the business world, as Puschmann and Burgess (2014) have shown. Given the significance of data in our public and everyday lives, many find the strong, confining link between data and business alarming; this is even more so, since data has gained societal and political importance through further technical developments in areas such as artificial intelligence (AI). As we will show in this text, recent advances in AI, particularly in the area of machine learning (ML; in which systems are trained on huge datasets), have opened up new possibilities for data analysis that have further strengthened the societal role of data in our political and social lives. This is why data needs to be understood more than ever not just as an economic opportunity but also as a *democratic frontier.*

When discussing data from the perspective of democracy, next to the rights of the individual and the effect of data on the individual, the effect of data on the collective, i.e., the shaping of a society, comes into view. Recently, a range of scholars have started to explore this *collective value of datasets* systematically and have shown that value for populations can be gained from insights into data relations emerging between individual data entries (Viljoen, 2021). This point is important,

DOI: 10.4324/9781003173427-3

as it highlights the power datasets have to drive benefits for societies (and not just companies), widely known as "data for the public good", which some argue could be governed by independent data trusts (see Delacroix, Pineau & Montgomery, 2021), a construct that is somewhat linked to the notion of digital commons (Dulong de Rosnay & Stalder, 2020). Such research into data trusts or digital commons stresses the collective value of data and calls for revisiting the principles of data governance, i.e., the processes that manage the *availability, usability* and *security* of data. Among these three aspects, it was the latter, the aspect of *security* and loss of privacy leading to a growing surveillance (Zuboff, 2019) that, at the beginning of the 21st century, gained most public attention with some positive effects. A variety of governments have tackled this issue by legislation amendments, one of the most far-reaching being Europe's General Data Protection Regulation (GDPR). The principles of *availability* and *usability*, however, were likewise discussed beyond experts and data science. Both principles have gained the attention of data activists, non-governmental organizations (NGOs) and even politicians – an attention that is now newly required. In his excellent genealogy of Open Data, Jonathan Gray (2014) has shown the wide range of initiatives Open Data has surfaced, from neoliberal takes to widening civic participation. Among them, we find calls for:

- opening data in a push for transparency to hold the public sector to account;
- reducing government by transforming it to a platform service;
- making data available that could be useful for businesses fostering economic growth and innovation;
- allowing citizens to reuse their data and/or to make their data portable from one platform to another; and
- making use of data to advance societal issues through civic hacking.

While the benefits and drawbacks of the above points are still being discussed, the focus on opening up data has recently shifted. This shift is an effect of two, at times overlapping, strands of research transforming data analysis profoundly: (1) the growing body of critical research into the bias of datasets and (2) the development of data analytics through the method of ML. Both strands put new attention on the *quality* of datasets, which has not only become essential but also opens up room for the creation of datasets as a societal tool with strong political potential, which is the focus of this chapter. And while there is a growing body of ethics codes in different domains (Stark &

Hoffmann, 2019) as well as calls for "data infrastructure literacy" (Gray et al., 2018), computational science has far too long neglected to focus on questions about the creation, composition and processing of data. In other words, despite calls to move toward critical data studies (Iliadis & Russo, 2016), much of our data practice, particularly regarding ML, has been kept invisible. Our chapter will show how this *invisibility*, which endangers the quality of data, could be challenged if we deployed *data solidarity* as a principle of governance for the creation of datasets; a principle that could help governments and corporations understand datasets not just as economic opportunities but also as democratic resources that offer possibilities to advance the public good.

On the Link between Data Quantity and Data Quality

Ever since digital technologies have transformed data to become what has been called "big data" (Kitchin, 2014) – i.e., extremely large data sets that can be analyzed computationally to reveal patterns, trends and associations – new opportunities but also profound challenges regarding the quality of datasets arose. Data has become a resource of social life leading to digital technology and sociality becoming tightly interwoven, at times inseparable (Marres, 2017: 7–44). With this, substantial problems around the quality of datasets and their handling became apparent and have started to be discussed by a wide range of scholars. Contributing to critical data science, danah boyd and Kate Crawford (2012: 666 and 668) have, e.g., shown that bigger data is not automatically better data and that early "claims to objectivity and accuracy" were misleading. Ruha Benjamin (2019: 127) has pointed out that datasets are often "naturally occurring" within digital industries and are therefore taken from contexts that "reflect deeply ingrained cultural prejudices and structural hierarchies". The far reach of those ingrained prejudices was further elaborated by Wendy Chun (2021: 17), who showed in her excellent study *Discriminating Data* that even when ML algorithms do not officially include race as a category, unbalanced datasets embed whiteness as a default. Besides racial bias, the digital sphere is also haunted by class (Schradie, 2011) and gender gaps, the latter exposed by Caroline Criado Perez (2019) describing the discrimination against women through data as systemic as there is an invisible bias with a profound effect on women's lives (e.g., there have long been life-threatening knowledge gaps within medical data about women's heart attacks which manifest in slightly different symptoms from men's on whom the research of this disease was long focused). Catherine D'Ignazio and Lauren F. Klein (2020) have also made a strong case showing example after example how profoundly data science needs feminism. Many of the above studies are interdisciplinary, drawing on important works within Computer Science such as the critical study into word embedding in natural language processing (Bolukbasi et al., 2016) or into the bias of large language models (Bender et al., 2021).

Being aware of such problems when gathering datasets or working with data is even more important in the face of ML developments advancing the capabilities of AI, which has widened the societal reach of data analysis. While cookies and other digital data traces allow for the predictive modeling of user data, i.e., informing conclusions and making predictions about those users, ML goes a step further. It can make predictions about users from *indirect* information, i.e., it is less dependent on data directly left about and by users. This is because of its new analytic capacity to process language, images or other symbols. Computational approaches to analyze these had long failed to succeed until ML using so-called "deep neural networks" allowed a breakthrough regarding the "calculation of meaning" (Bunz, 2019; Cantwell Smith, 2021), meaning which users accidentally leave behind when speaking, writing or appearing in photos or videos. Processing these formats and calculating meaning signified by them is a new capacity of data analysis that substantially widens the data pool as it allows reaching out much wider in the analysis of user information. The effect of ML is therefore a profoundly deeper reach of digital technology into the fabric of our societies, thereby affecting its social and political processes.

To gain this reach, large datasets featuring our audio, video, photos or written texts are used to train ML systems, whereby the configuration and quality of data plays an essential role to train them correctly. At the same time, there has been a lack of attention regarding datasets due to the fact that in computer science, their creation (such as, e.g., the ImageNet dataset; Deng et al., 2009) has long been valued less than the making of algorithms or the building of models. The reason for this is that gathering or acquiring a dataset is, strictly speaking, not a computational procedure. Many introductory books teaching ML in computer science assume datasets as already available (e.g., Alpaydin, 2020: 154; Flach, 2012; Witten et al., 2011) making their creation an "invisible practice". However, acquiring a dataset for training is *fundamental to the development of machine learning models*, which is why critical knowledge about the quality of data needs to become a standard in practices, from the conception to deployment of ML. While data is not a computational procedure, the actual workflow when constructing a neural network to perform ML begins with the acquisition of a dataset, as Jaton showed in great detail in his ethnographic study of a computer science laboratory (2021: 54): for ML models, obtaining a dataset is part of "the practical processes that enable them to come into existence" (11). In other words, datasets are essential to train ML models; an observation that in 2021 led Andrew Ng, Professor at Stanford University Department of Computer Science and Electrical Engineering, to call for a more "data-centric AI" (Ng 2021). High-quality data, however, is not sufficiently publicly available to ML developers, and this is often highlighted as one of the biggest issues in the field. The essential role described here for datasets and their quality regarding ML, and with that the even bigger importance datasets have come to play in the technical and political realities of our overdeveloped world, creates the need for a different approach toward data: an approach that needs to engage with the issues of critical data science (Iliadis & Russo, 2016) in face of the fact that processing data creates and deprives opportunities. By revealing the absences, differences and disconnects within datasets, we can address some of the sociocultural problems they create. These issues show why a critical conceptualization that aims to make data more fair, transparent, available and accountable for the community is needed so we can think of "data as a public good".

The concept of "data as a public good" has been developed as a response to the massive deployment of data analytics by technology companies such as Google or Palantir. As Lane et al. (2014) point out in the introduction of *Privacy, big data, and the public good*, one of the first books on this topic:

> Much has been made of the many uses of (…) data for pragmatic purposes, including selling goods and services, winning political campaigns, and identifying possible terrorists. Yet big data can also be harnessed to serve the public good in other ways: scientists can use new forms of data to do research that improves the lives of human beings; federal, state, and local governments can use data to improve services and reduce taxpayer costs; and public organizations can use information to advocate for public causes, for example.
>
> (Lane et al., 2014: XI)

However, in an increasingly datafied world, the systemic and structural inequities we described earlier are intensified and exacerbated by narrow conceptions of how datasets are produced, reproduced, combined and shared. Data structures and data processes such as the building of new datasets through other datasets, the combination of data etc. (see Roberts et al., 2021) are *invisible processes* that impact every decision that is taken based on their analysis. And these *invisible data processes*, mounded on existing systemic and structural inequities, can have profound societal consequences. In other words, *invisible data processes*, such as non-accessible, non-structured, non-available or misrepresented, incomplete or biased data often impact specific populations and countries, and are a threat to the health and safety of the global public. As Roberts points out, invisibility is "a metaphor that figures a state of being that comes into existence when others refuse to see us, to acknowledge our existence, to accept our presence as making a contribution to a world of meaning" (Roberts, 1999: 121). He goes on to argue that invisibility is not just created systemically and structurally, but it is also sustained through the complicity of those who are invisibilized – and this is why data solidarity, as we are going to show, is so important. Applying this logic to the invisibilization of data, it becomes clear that if we act as if data processes are visible, we perpetuate this invisibilization and sustain the power structures that suppress and marginalize data and their societal impact. How can we balance the fears of data/public control from Big Tech with the significance of data for the betterment of sectors such as healthcare? A challenge that translates into: how can we do good with better and more data? By now, several definitions aim to conceptualize this different political approach to data ranging from data justice (Dencik et al., 2016), responsible data (van der Aalst et al., 2017) to the call for data trusts (Delacroix, Pineau & Montgomery, 2021). To this, we would like to add the concept of *data solidarity* and the need to overcome the invisibility of data practice. In the following, we will demonstrate a need for this through a case study.

Case Study: On the Role of Datasets for Machine Learning Research

To understand the importance of data processes and cut through their invisibility, we studied the role datasets have for ML research in healthcare, particularly the usage of patient data to train ML systems. Taking advantage of the abundance of ML models being trained and developed within healthcare, we conducted a systematic literature search focused on medical diagnosis on arXiv; arXiv, hosted by Cornell University, was chosen as it plays a central role for the publication of research by the ML community (Balki et al., 2019). Established in 1990, the repository is generally a popular place of prepublication for science, technology, engineering and mathematics (STEM) disciplines as it has a fast publishing turnaround getting papers out before peer review (Delfanti, 2016); the pace in which ML research develops created the need for researchers to get their findings out quickly. Our systematic literature research focuses on a very specific area – that of ML models assisting with medical diagnosis. On arXiv, 82 relevant studies were identified by searching "machine learning", "medical", "diagnostics". One duplicate was removed with the use of reference management software. The remaining papers were included if they met the criteria of describing a ML experiment in a scientific paper that involved processing medical data entries. This led to a corpus of 62 papers published between 2009 and 2021 that were analyzed in detail regarding their usage of data. Our aim was to learn more about the medical datasets used when training and validating ML models, a process that is in parts invisibilized – while datasets are mentioned, their creation is often treated as negligible. The focus was therefore on the origin and the creation of a dataset, including the gathering and (in some cases for supervised learning) on the labeling of data, information that at times is communicated in the margins (through acknowledgements, affiliations, etc.). Cleaning of existing datasets was not taken into account. Datasets mentioned in the papers were coded according to three categories: Code N for *newly created datasets*; code L for *datasets that had to be labeled* by medical experts to allow for supervised learning; code P for *publicly available datasets*.

We found that over half of the experiments, 33 papers, worked with publicly available datasets, i.e., medical datasets that have been published to foster research such as the National Institutes of Health Chest X-Ray Dataset published by the National Library of Medicine in the US, or the Alzheimer's Disease Neuroimaging Initiative (ADNI). Six further experiments used datasets of mixed status, i.e., some were publicly available while others were specifically created for the study. This procedure reflects the process of training a ML system, which runs through two or three interlinked phases each needing separate datasets – the phase of training the ML model (1) and of testing the model (2b); some also validate the model with a step in the middle adjusting parameters further (2a). About a third, 21 experiments, created their own dataset from the ground up; all but one through a close collaboration with a medical institution.

Even though the findings of this systematic review are not representative, they clearly show a strong tendency within ML research: The majority of experiments, 33 out of 62 papers, used publicly available datasets. Adding the six experiments that made use of available datasets while enriching them with newly created ones, one could come to the conclusion that 39 papers, i.e. 63% of the papers we reviewed, worked with available datasets. Given the fact that publicly available datasets are rare, this clearly shows the extent to which datasets incentivize and influence the conducting of ML research – they are obviously needed. And this is the case for academic research as well as for businesses. Among our body of 62 papers were six in which businesses led the research or were part of it – some big ones such as Google Brain or Microsoft Research plus a range of less well-known, smaller companies. Most of them were working with available datasets: among the 39 papers using publicly available datasets, five were conducted by businesses or in collaboration with businesses. Only one paper, for which academics collaborated with the British company Babylon Health, used a newly created dataset, most likely one Babylon Health held internally.

The demand for publicly available datasets clearly shows their potential. Datasets strongly incentivize both academic and commercial research. Despite the talk of big data, however, they are scarce – platforms such as Kaggle, which allows users to find and publish data sets and was bought by Google in 2017, lists 50,000 datasets for more than one million active users. This indicates that in 2021, too many users conducting data analysis research worked with the same datasets, which our analysis confirmed. A dataset from the Alzheimer's Disease Neuroimaging Initiative (ADNI) was used five times in papers from Russia, France, US, Pakistan and China. Overall, publicly available datasets such as ADNI or the chest X-ray datasets published by the National Institute of Health and others led to multiple papers using them. Papers frequently mentioned that "progress has been hindered by a sparsity of available training data, commonly attributed to the difficulty of publishing datasets" (McManigle et al., 2020: 1) or noted that "in domains where data is highly regulated and expert time is rare, it can be exceedingly cumbersome to obtain new expert-labeled data sets every time a model needs to be improved" (Cai et al., 2019: 12). As Roberts et al. (2021) have also pointed out, the need for public data leads to serious issues for research. More and more datasets are "assembled from other datasets and redistributed under a new name". These "Frankenstein datasets" may inadvertently include overlapping or identical datasets, which, in turn, lead algorithms to wrong diagnoses and suggestions.

The scarcity of data and the invisible data processes that produce datasets lead to working with unbalanced datasets – an issue that impacts not just the medical but all sectors, and with it, society. While data is abundant, the majority of datasets are proprietary and built for commercial reasons with no oversight. At the same time, as demonstrated by the high number of Kaggle users compared to the low number of public datasets, publicly available datasets are generally scarce. While the issue is known, the low regard for the creation of datasets, which, as we have shown, is often not seen as an act of computer engineering and not taught in introductory ML books, makes the need for public datasets pertinent.

This is where an approach foregrounding the democratic value of data and an initiative to create datasets making them publicly available out of a gesture of *solidarity* could help. This is even more the case, as in current debates, the focus on the *collective value* datasets have for society is often missing (Delacroix & Montgomery, 2020; Viljoen 2021). This is worrying as data analysis, driven further by ML, has become a process people experience directly or indirectly everyday: when shopping on the internet, when using government services or when applying for a loan or an insurance. As long as these data analysis decisions are based on commercial datasets without checks and balances and to which there is no alternative, there will be issues of bias and fairness leading to a lack of trust. This importance of taking the collective value of data into perspective has been demonstrated by Salome Viljoen (2021). In her in-depth report on the issue titled "Democratic Data", she correctly reminds readers:

> The data economy has resulted in massive collection of information regarding consumer purchasing preferences and social networks, for instance, but has contributed comparatively little to ongoing discussions concerning waste production, water usage, or how wealth from financial instruments flows globally.
>
> (649)

With the understanding of big data as something mainly useful for business, data to support our democratic public infrastructures needs further strengthening. Admittedly, the change needed here is not just infrastructural, it is also political. A democratic use of data could tackle bias in datasets and handle it more transparently; it could turn toward opportunities such as programmes to create datasets in under-researched areas that are socially relevant or help us understand niche issues that have been consistently ignored due to lack of corporate or government interest. As Viljoen points out: "Datafication is not only unjust because data extraction or resulting datafied governmentality may violate individual autonomy; datafication may also be unjust because it violates ideals of social equality" (58). Viljoen calls for a shift in the understanding of data "from an individual medium expressing individual interests, to a democratic medium that materializes population-level, social interests" (54). This would also mean the following:

-   data does not only need to be gathered where it naturally occurs, instead governments need to start initiating the collection of datasets to ensure democratic values;
-   datasets could be used to allow citizens a better representation in the conditions and purposes of data production;
-   issues with bias in datasets can be targeted or made transparent;
-   datasets could be used to incentivize ML research in particular areas attractive from a societal and not commercial perspective.

These points, however, depend on the availability of data and the willingness of citizens to embrace data sharing for the public good. Naturally, the gaining of data for the public good operates differently from the commercial top-down approach leading to data extraction. Instead, it must revolve from a participatory understanding of data sharing and a belief in "data commons". This needs communicative work. As Dulong de Rosnay and Stalder have (2020: 16) pointed out:

> The constitution of data commons (...) needs to overcome the apparent contradiction between personal data and property, and between privacy and open access, as a personal data commons would not lead to sharing personal information, but to govern their reuse according to values of the digital commons.

This brings the importance of solidarity, exercised by giving data to support the community, to the fore.

Toward Data Solidarity

In order to develop not just fair and transparent but also democratic and visible data processes, we propose that we need to cultivate and sustain a culture of solidarity in data sharing processes. Solidarity has functioned as a key principle in democratic struggles of the past, such as the labor union Polish Solidarność of the 1980s, the mid-19th-century French workers' fight against oppression (Wilde, 2013) and in the most recent past, in social movements such as Occupy (Vrikki, 2018). In social movements, solidarity visibilizes and materializes values such as trust, openness and common principles (Pavan & della Porta, 2020). In the data era we currently experience, living with others and the social construction of our societies have given solidarity a wider role that does not just hold political importance, it can also be perceived as a form of caring and protecting others (Chatzidakis et al., 2020). At the same time, this can build on interpretations of solidarity in social theory where one finds, on the one hand, interpretations that perceive solidarity as the sum of norms contributing to social cohesion, e.g., in the works of Emilé Durkheim (1984, 2001), and on the other hand, one finds interpretations that deduce solidarity as a relationship between members of a group with common interests, referring to the works of Marx (1906) and Weber (1978). Beyond social theory, political philosopher Scholz (2008) has identified three kinds of solidarity: social solidarity (describing the relationship between the group), civic solidarity (referring to the relationship between citizens and the state) and political solidarity (expressing the commitment and morals of the individual), which divide solidarity based on the relationships onto which it depends on. The variety of approaches within social and political theory shows how ingrained solidarity is in our social, political and cultural lives that in everyday life gets often translated as the process of supporting the vulnerable, as acts of public caring such as education, welfare and healthcare and as the primary care relations we build and sustain through friendships, households and families (Lynch, 2007).

Building on these interpretations and approaches, we identify *data solidarity* as an articulation of *visibilizing data processes* for the benefit of public good. The proposition here is to perceive data solidarity in a productive opposition to current hierarchical data structures as well as to the latent processes of the neoliberal market, personal responsibility and individual agency (Cohen, 2010). This is pertinent to the conceptualization of data processes as a set of democratic norms that together reinforce the capacity of communities to produce collective goods for the public benefit (Laitinen & Pessi, 2014). Recent critical studies into the democratisation of AI, for example by Himmelreich (2021), have stressed that the matter is complicated and that there is no simple administrative panacea to the injustices that are perpetuated by AI. Attention towards ways, in which democratic governance of AI can be initiated and structured, are still underdeveloped. Informed by these reasons, we propose 'data solidarity' as a value supporting a process to enhance our AI futures in the same way solidarity between working class and farmers resulted in the establishment of a universal pension system (Baldwin, 1990). Data solidarity can advance the inclination of corporate and public data stakeholders to share both the risks and the benefits of data access, production and sharing. The term solidarity is "sometimes used as a nebulous concept" (Stjernø, 2009: 2), but data solidarity can most conducively be defined as the willingness to share datasets and resources with others while acknowledging the invisible processes that take place during the creation, production and sharing of datasets. Visibilizing those processes and their flaws that may result in marginalizations such as racism, sexism and classism accentuate the need for a collective action that will be based on the values or solidarity.

Conclusion: Moving from Big to Democratic Data

In the same ways in which our political and financial systems have determined so much of our behaviors and societies, data analytics are and will keep stretching our cultures and democracy. In this chapter, we aim to answer this challenge by making the political force of data practices visible. Our argument positions itself as an addition to the ongoing debate about *critical data practice*, which aims "to account for, inventively respond to and intervene around the socio-technical infrastructures involved in the creation, extraction and analysis of data" (Gray et al., 2018: 8). Our research also builds on recent insights into collective aspects regarding datasets (Delacroix, Pineau & Montgomery, 2021; Viljoen, 2021), insights that (a) are gained *from the collective*, i.e., from relations between data entries, and could (b) be processed *for the collective* advancing the public good. To advance this, the tendency to shroud data practice in invisibility needs to end. To move from big to democratic data, we need to understand datasets and data infrastructure as democratic tools which can advance societal interests and assist with bringing forth elements of public good for populations. How influential publicly available datasets are, could be seen in our case study of medical diagnosis through ML systems trained on medical data. To encourage the building of such publicly available datasets, we need a new notion of data: next to the understandable fear about surveillance through the extraction of data, we need to stress the potential that data sharing has in public hands and move toward data solidarity. While there is no simple answer to the question "how can we do good with better and more data?", we know that ultimately it boils down to collective action. By deploying *solidarity as a principle of data governance* for the creation of publicly held datasets, we can start building trust and accountability. Digital technologies, AI systems such as ML and other advanced data analytics can help us better our societies if we deploy principles of critical data practice that visibilize data processes and apply a critical approach to datasets aiming for the inclusion of different kinds of data. As we stand at the precipice of datafied democracy, now is an opportunity for a steady refocus on how data and data infrastructure can support inclusion. The data infrastructures we shape, shape us in return. The rise of AI has made these infrastructures even more important. To shape these infrastructures according to democratic values, the principle of data solidarity is essential.

We would like to express our thanks to Shuprima Guha, Jonathan Gray and Adam Bull for their useful comments and corrections.

Bibliography

Alpaydin, E. (2020). *Introduction to machine learning.* Cambridge, MA: MIT press.

Baldwin, P. (1990). *The politics of social solidarity: Class bases of the European Welfare State, 1875–1975.* Cambridge: Cambridge University Press.

Balki, I., Amirabadi, A., Levman, J., Martel, A. L., Emersic, Z., Meden, B., Garcia-Pedrero, A., Ramirez, S. C., Kong, D., Moody, A. R., & Tyrrell, P. N. (2019). "Sample-size determination methodologies for machine learning in medical imaging research: A systematic review." *Canadian Association of Radiologists Journal*, 70(4): 344–353.

Bender, E. M., Gebru, T., McMillan-Major, A., & Shmitchell, S. (2021, March). On the dangers of stochastic parrots: Can language models be too big? In *Proceedings of the 2021 ACM Conference on Fairness, Accountability, and Transparency*: 610–623.

Benjamin, R. (2019). *Race after technology: Abolitionist tools for the new jim code.* Cambridge: Polity.

Bolukbasi, T., Chang, K. W., Zou, J., Saligrama, V., & Kalai, A. (2016). Quantifying and reducing stereotypes in word embeddings. *arXiv preprint arXiv*:1606.06121.

Boyd, D., & Crawford, K. (2012). Critical questions for big data: Provocations for a cultural, technological, and scholarly phenomenon. *Information, Communication & Society*, 15(5): 662–679.

Bunz, M. (2019). The calculation of meaning: On the misunderstanding of new artificial intelligence as culture. *Culture, Theory and Critique*, 60(3–4): 264–278.

Cai, C. J., Reif, E., Hegde, N., Hipp, J., Kim, B., Smilkov, D., & Terry, M. (2019, May). Human-centered tools for coping with imperfect algorithms during medical decision-making. In *Proceedings of the 2019 CHI Conference on Human Factors in Computing Systems*, 1–14.

Cantwell Smith, B. (2021, April). The foundations and metaphysic of computing [draft]. NYU Digital Theory Lab.

Chatzidakis, A., Hakim, J., Littler, J., Rottenberg, C., & Segal, L. (2020). From carewashing to radical care: The discursive explosions of care during Covid-19. *Feminist Media Studies*, 20(6): 889–895.

Chun, W. H. K., (2021) *Discriminating data*. Cambridge, MA: MIT Press.

Cohen, C. J. (2010). *Democracy remixed: Black youth and the future of American politics*. New York: Oxford University Press.

Delacroix, S., Pineau, J., & Montgomery, J. (2021). Democratising the digital revolution: The role of data governance. In: Braunschweig, B. & Ghallab, M. (ed.) *Reflections on AI for Humanity* (pp. 1–15). Cham: Springer.

Delacroix, S., & Montgomery, J. (2020). From research data ethics principles to practice: Data trusts as a governance tool. *Available at SSRN 3736090*.

Delfanti, A. (2016). Beams of particles and papers: How digital preprint archives shape authorship and credit, *Social Studies of Science*, 46(4): 629–645.

Dencik, L., Hintz, A., & Cable, J. (2016). Towards data justice? The ambiguity of anti-surveillance resistance in political activism. *Big Data & Society*, 3(2): 2053951716679678.

Deng, J., Dong, W., Socher, R., Li, L. J., Li, K., & Fei-Fei, L. (2009, June). Imagenet: A large-scale hierarchical image database. In *2009 IEEE conference on computer vision and pattern recognition* (pp. 248–255). IEEE.

D'ignazio, C., & Klein, L. F. (2020). *Data feminism*. Cambridge, MA: MIT press.

Dulong de Rosnay, M., & Stalder, F. (2020). Digital commons. *Internet Policy Review*, 9(4): 1–22, http://dx.doi.org/10.14763/2020.4.1530

Durkheim, E. (1984 [1983]). *The division of labor in society*. Translated by Q. D. Halls with an Introduction by Lewis Coser. New York: Free Press.

Durkheim, E. (2001[1912]). *The elementary forms of religious life. A new translation by Carol Cosman*. Oxford: Oxford University Press.

Flach, P. (2012). *Machine learning: The art and science of algorithms that make sense of data*. Cambridge: Cambridge University Press.

Gray, J. Towards a genealogy of open data (September 3, 2014). The paper was given at the *General Conference of the European Consortium for Political Research in Glasgow*, 3–6th September 2014. http://dx.doi.org/10.2139/ssrn.2605828

Gray, J., Gerlitz, C., & Bounegru, L. (2018). Data infrastructure literacy. *Big Data & Society*. https://doi.org/10.1177/2053951718786316

Himmelreich, J. (2021). Against 'democratizing AI'. Forthcoming in *AI & Society*. https://johanneshimmelreich.net/papers/against-democratizing-AI.pdf

Iliadis, A., & Russo, F. (2016). Critical data studies: An introduction. *Big Data & Society*, 3(2). https://doi.org/10.1177/2053951716674238.

Jaton, F. (2021). *The constitution of algorithms: Ground-truthing, programming, formulating*. Cambridge, MA: MIT Press.

Kitchin, R. (2014). Big Data, new epistemologies and paradigm shifts. *Big Data & Society*, 1(1) https://doi.org/10.1177/2053951714528481.

Laitinen, A., & Pessi, A. B. (2014). *Solidarity: Theory and practice. An introduction*. Minneapolis, MN: Lexington Books.

Lane, J., Stodden, V., Bender, S., & Nissenbaum, H. (Eds.). (2014). *Privacy, big data, and the public good: Frameworks for engagement.* New York: Cambridge University Press.

Lynch, K. (2007). Love labour as a distinct and non-commodifiable form of care labour. *Sociological Review*, 54(3): 550–570.

Marres, N. (2017). *Digital sociology: The reinvention of social research.* Cambridge, UK: Polity Press.

Marx, K. (1906). *Capital*, Vol. 1. Translated by S. Moore, E. B. Aveling and E. Untermann. New York: Modern Library.

McManigle, J. E., Bartz, R. R., & Carin, L. (2020, July). Y-Net for Chest X-Ray preprocessing: Simultaneous classification of geometry and segmentation of annotations. In 2020 42nd Annual International Conference of the IEEE Engineering in Medicine & Biology Society (EMBC) (pp. 1266–1269). *IEEE.*

Ng, A. (2021) MLOps: From model-centric to data-centric AI. *Deeplearning.ai* https://www.deeplearning.ai/wp-content/uploads/2021/06/MLOps-From-Model-centric-to-Data-centric-AI.pdf

Pavan, E., & della Porta, D. (2020). Social movements, communication, and media. In Lievrouw, L. A., & Loader, B. D. (Eds.). *Routledge Handbook of Digital Media and Communication* (pp. 307–318). New York: Routledge.

Perez, C. C. (2019). *Invisible women: Exposing data bias in a world designed for men.* London: Penguin Random House.

Puschmann, C., & Burgess, J. (2014). Metaphors of big data. *International Journal of Communication*, 8: 1690–1709.

Roberts, J. W. (1999). "… Hidden right out in the open": The field of folklore and the problem of invisibility 1998 American Folklore Society presidential address. *Journal of American Folklore*, 112(444) (Spring, 1999): 119–139.

Roberts, M., Driggs, D., Thorpe, M. et al. (2021). Common pitfalls and recommendations for using machine learning to detect and prognosticate for COVID-19 using chest radiographs and CT scans. *Natural Machine Intelligence*, 3: 199–217.

Scholz, S. J. (2008). *Political solidarity.* Pennsylvania, USA: Penn State Press.

Schradie, J. (2011). The digital production gap: The digital divide and Web 2.0 collide. *Poetics*, 39(2): 145–168.

Stark, L., & Hoffmann, A. L. (2019). Data is the new what? Popular metaphors & professional ethics in emerging data culture. *Journal of Cultural Analytics.* https://doi.org/10.22148/16.036

Stjernø, S. (2009). *Solidarity in Europe: The history of an idea.* New York: Cambridge University Press.

van der Aalst, W. M. P., Bichler, M., & Heinzl, A. (2017). Responsible data science. *Business & Information Systems Engineering*, 59: 311.

Viljoen, S. (2021, November). A relational theory for data governance. *Yale Law Journal*, 131(2), 573–645.

Vrikki, P. (2018). The beginning of the end: Telling the story of Occupy Wall Street's eviction on Twitter. In Adi A. (ed.) *Protest public relations: Communicating dissent and activism* (pp. 76–93). London: Routledge.

Weber, M. (1978). *Economy and society: An outline of interpretive sociology* (Vol. 1). Berkeley: University of California Press.

Wilde, L. (2013). *Global solidarity.* Edinburgh: Edinburgh University Press.

Witten, I., Frank, E., & Hall, M. (2011). *Data mining: Practical machine learning tools and techniques.* Amsterdam: Elsevier.

Zuboff, S. (2019). *The age of surveillance capitalism: The fight for a human future at the new frontier of power.* New York: Public Affairs.

4 Democratic Possibilities of Digital Feminism

The Case of #Istanbul ConventionSavesLives and #IstanbulSozlesmesi

Kristin Comeforo and Berna Görgülü

On July 16, 2020, Pınar Gültekin, a 27-year-old university student disappeared from the town where she lives. Five days later, her body was found in the forest. She was brutally beaten and strangled to death by her former partner, Cemal Metin Avcı, who then put her body in a barrel, burned it, and poured concrete over it. She was just one among the 36 women murdered in Turkey in July 2020.

Pinar's murder created a perfect storm that raged around women in Turkey. For one, at least one woman had been killed almost every day in Turkey at the time – often perpetrated by current or former romantic partners (Şimşek, 2019). At the same time, there had been a growing movement within some conservative corners to leave the Istanbul Convention, which is a human rights treaty focused on preventing and combating violence against women.[1] The Convention has been instrumental in saving women's lives in signatory countries and has thus been a substantial success for democratic struggles, namely those engaged by global feminism.

In response to this storm, feminists in Turkey began using the #ChallengeAccepted and #IstanbulConventionSavesLives hashtags on social media to stand in solidarity with victims, provide a counter narrative to the femininity of women in Turkey, and pressure the government to enforce the laws of the Istanbul Convention. Rather than enforcing the laws, the Turkish government withdrew from the convention completely on June 30, 2021.

Despite digital feminism's failure to influence the Turkish government's decision, a growing body of scholarship suggests that the value and impact of digital activism cannot be judged by concrete legal and policy changes alone (Mendes et al., 2019). This inspires us to investigate the uses, roles, and impact of social media in the democratic

DOI: 10.4324/9781003173427-4

struggle for women's rights in the illiberal, authoritarian country of Turkey. New media technologies foster democracy through affordances, such as reaching larger audiences through different media tools, enriching diversity of voices, adjusting the language and goals of the struggle according to people's priorities, and taking the struggle beyond borders. These affordances are reflective of feminist values and thus draw connective lines between feminism as a form of democratic struggle and new media technologies as platforms for both. Will these affordances "translate" for feminists in Turkey, whose movement has been shaped by an institutionalized and "mediated misogyny" (Vickery & Everbach, 2018) that is so committed to the murder of women that the country does not keep official statistics on femicide (Kucukgocmen & Utsa, 2021)?

In this chapter, we focus on #ChallengeAccepted and #IstanbulConventionSavesLives because these hashtags invited the world to join the struggle against femicide, raised consciousness around violence against women in Turkey, and yet failed to win protections for this endangered class. By connecting this case to other studies and scholarly literature around digital organizing, digital activism, and digital feminisms, we identified structural aspects that suggest these hashtags operated as an ecosystem, which included complex networks of power and mediation, and that the greatest value of this form of hashtag activism may lie beyond legislative, policy, and/or legal changes.

Democracy and Digital Media

Communication has always played a central role in social justice movements from their emergence and formation (Bennett & Segerberg, 2015), through their organizing for collective action (Waisbord, 2011) and to their actual mobilization of the masses (Martin, 2015). Communication has also been critical for providing legitimacy to the movement (Bennett & Segerberg, 2015), which increases its influence on public opinion and decision-makers (Waisbord, 2011).

In the past, activists were limited to traditional media, which are largely controlled by government, law enforcement officers, corporate, or other elite actors whose interests are antithetical to those of activists (Herman & Chomsky, 1988). With the addition of the new digital media, today's social movements enjoy a hybrid ecology and a broader spectrum of choices (Treré, 2018) among platforms that spread control and production among users, the activists themselves (Castells, 2012). Digital and social media provide several technological affordances that are useful to and promote digital activism: "persistence, replicability, scalability, and searchability" (Papacharissi, 2015); partial anonymity, visibility, and association/connectivity (Treem & Leonardi, 2013); instantaneous, real-time forms of communication that can be one-to-many, one-to-one, and many-to-many (Cammaerts, 2015); the construction of collective identity (Khazraee & Novak, 2018); and inclusiveness and direct participation (Kavada, 2016). These affordances provide "new dynamics for amplifying, recording, and spreading information and social acts" (Khazraee & Novak, 2018, p. 3), which are integral for social movements.

Affordances vary by platform, and each has developed its own "vernacular" (Cho, 2015; Gibbs et al, 2015; Warfield, 2016) that reflects and shapes how it is best used by activists. Amnesty International Australia (2020), for instance, reports that Facebook is "great for" sharing information, amplifying the voices of others, and creating community; while Instagram is great for visual communication that demonstrates the size and scale of the movement, while grabbing attention; and Twitter is best for keeping up with "in the moment" news and information and direct contact with one another. Additional platforms and tools, such as group text messaging through applications like WhatsApp, also excel in direct contact capability. WhatsApp's end-to-end encryption of messages makes it far more secure than email and SMS (mobile text messaging) (What's App, 2021) and has thus made it one of activists' most favored communication technologies.

Despite these affordances, the democratic possibilities of digital media technologies remain up for debate. "Initial optimism" of the internet as a democratizing force that opens wider spaces for deliberation via a virtual public sphere has been tempered by a "second wave" of discourse that recognizes how these new technologies are products of systems of power and oppression and are thus incapable of developing democratic values (Iosifidis & Wheeler, 2015). WhatsApp, social media platforms, and the internet as a whole have been "shut down" by governments during unrest and protests in Zimbabwe in 2016 (Shapshak, 2016), in India in 2018, and Pakistan in 2021, to highlight just a few instances.

Similarly, the corporate ownership of most, if not all, of these platforms impacts what content gets seen by users and what is promoted. Algorithms are set to maximize profits, which are largely generated through advertising and sponsor revenue. Concentration of ownership, profit orientation, and dedication to serving the interests of elites are key attributes of media under neoliberalism (Herman & Chomsky, 1988). Neoliberalism is the sociopolitical-economic theory associated with free market capitalism, which removes all obstacles to the accumulation of capital by calling for privatization of industry, deregulation, globalization, and free trade, removal of state-sponsored social services, and shifting responsibility to/focus on the individual.

The cult of individuality has shaped all aspects of social life, from the way we engage with friends, family, and co-workers to how we make purchase decisions and life choices. Critics of neoliberalism argue that this hyper-individuality depoliticizes citizenry and replaces civic duty with consumerism. This issue is heightened by the consolidation of new digital media and new social movements into what Flesher Fominaya and Gillan (2017) call the *technology-media-movement complex.* Ideology, hierarchy, and inequality abound in digital activism, with groups that are more hierarchical and bureaucratic – often thought of as the antithesis of democratic – possessing the infrastructure to develop and maintain online engagement (Schradie, 2014). Power ensures that certain movement groups will dictate the tenor and tactics of the broader movement, and that issues will be oversimplified by communication networks that reinforce, rather than challenge, neoliberal capitalist and colonialist ideas (Iosifidis & Wheeler, 2015; Khoja-Moolji, 2015).

In terms of social movements and activism, this complicates and constrains the route of messaging and forces a radical rethinking of the meaning of collective action and political agency (Kavada, 2016). In this way, Bennett and Segerberg (2013) encourage us to consider digital media as "connective" rather than collective. These connections, made possible by digital and social media, elevate the solitary acts of "sitting at the computer or tapping on our phones" to collective social movement activism (Mendes et al., 2019, p. 186). This mental image – of the individual alone at a keyboard – reminds us that in the case of digital media and activism, the medium may not be the message. "Digital media are neither a revolutionary driver nor a cause of protest" (Lim, 2018, p. 103), and they do "not contain the agency to effect social change" (Papacharissi, 2015). Still, digital media are useful to activists, thanks to the many affordances they provide, and it is through this use – to "renegotiate what is considered private and what is considered public in public life" (Papacharissi, 2015) – that the media acquire their agency. This "renegotiation" and agency, however, is not equally distributed and/or accessible across societies. Intersectionality reminds us that gender, race, and class – among other lived experiences – overlap and interact to produce a web of oppressions (and privileges) that come to bear on people to varying degrees. Digital feminism further takes up the issue of intersectionality.

Digital Feminism

Digital media did not only thoroughly change how organizations and movements structure their communication practices, but it also shifted and is still shifting the texture of movements themselves. One movement that has found new life and new tactics through digital and social media is feminism. In fact, Mendes et al. (2018) observed that the public's willingness to resist and challenge sexism increased, just as feminist uptake of digital communication increased (p. 237).

This recent rise of feminist sentiment and activity through digital technologies and the internet has been dubbed "fourth-wave feminism" by some, which is still a shadowy, yet captivating, silhouette (Baumgardner, 2011). The existence and efficacy of a feminist "fourth wave" has been challenged by those who maintain that not only is increased usage of the internet not enough to delineate a new feminist era (Munro, 2013), but also that digitally mediated activism lacks the ability to "truly make change occur" (Meyer & Workman Bray, 2013). Further, critics also call attention to the web of power, politics, and profits that govern the internet and produce an insecure environment for digital feminism (Yilmaz, 2017). They assert that neoliberalism's entanglement with this new kind of "popular" or "post" feminism indicates a reconciliation with capitalism, which is ontologically contradictory to feminism (Banet-Weiser et al., 2020). In this way, digital feminism or the supposed fourth wave focuses on the individual self rather than systemic sexism, and thus fundamentally thins down the movement's capacity to generate change (Banet-Weiser et al., 2020).

Despite these criticisms, it is hard to overlook how the internet has enabled mass political participation (Yilmaz, 2017) and how it has played a unique role in building solidarity among women and producing "communities of conversation" (Mendes et al., 2018) that are integral for local and global movements. More specifically, the internet has created a "call-out" culture (Mendes et al., 2019), in which sexism or misogyny can be "called out" – so its structural and systemic nature is exposed – and challenged. While it is true that most digital feminism activism does not result in tangible changes to policies or laws, Mendes et al. (2019) encourage us to value the affective benefits of the practice, which "directly changes and shapes the experiences, interactions, expectations, and views of our participants' everyday lives in profound ways" (p. 30).

As neither the first nor the last, #ChallengeAccepted and #IstanbulConventionSavesLives join a global digital feminist movement that is indeed changing and shaping women's everyday lives in powerful

ways. Hashtag feminism creates a widespread collectivity around issues and problems (Khoja-Moolji, 2015), while the internet and social
media provide sites for "feminist virtual consciousness raising," where
self-expression, sharing, interaction, and dialogue (hooks, 2000) work
to make the personal, political (Hanisch, 1969). Feminist hashtags have
risen from different corners of the world and are networked across
the globe through the rallying cries of #MeToo, #WhyIStayed, and
#BeenRapedNeverReported, among others. #MeToo, for instance,
was a call for women to break their silence around their experiences of
rape and sexual assault. According to Fox and Diehm (2017):

> To date, there have been more than 2.3 million #MeToo tweets
> from 85 countries; on Facebook, more than 24 million people par-
> ticipated in the conversation by posting, reacting, and comment-
> ing over 77 million times since October 15[,2017].

As part of #MeToo's global movement, French speakers proclaimed
#BalanceTonPorc, Spanish speakers #YoTambien, Italians #Quella-
VoltaChe, and Arabic speakers in countries like Egypt shared through
#أنا_كمان ("Ana kaman") (Lekach, 2017). Mendes et al. (2018) note how
digital technologies and culture not only "makes feminist activism
possible" (p. 240) but also that hashtags produce "communities of conversation" (p. 237) that transcend borders. Further, in countries like
Saudi Arabia, where the feminist mobilization of women is restricted
by laws and sociopolitical culture, because it threatens to society and
the cohesion of "family values," digital feminist activism becomes the
only "safe" option for activists (Alsahi, 2018, p. 317).

Unlike offline activism, which is unable to hide the bodies and identities of activists and thus opens women to the physical and social
dangers of being visible, digital platforms become possible safe ha-
vens by offering anonymity and physical distance. The possibilities for
safe activist spaces rarely materialize, and illustrate the double-edged
sword of digital affordances – while it has allowed for a "popular"
feminism to grow, it has also allowed a parallel "popular misogyny" to
grow, "as a structural force, [that] is networked, expressed, and prac-
ticed on multiple platforms, [and] attracting other like-minded groups
and individuals" (Banet-Weiser, 2018, p. 13). Misogyny isn't just the
hatred of women, "it is the instrumentalization of women as objects,
where women are a means to an end, a systematic devaluing and dehu-
manizing of women that takes place in a network and on a network"
(Banet-Weiser, 2019, p. 76). As a result of this "mediated misogyny"
(Vickery & Everbach, 2018), it is typical for feminists or women

speaking out against oppression and structural sexism/misogyny to get rape and death threats and/or to be "doxxed" (have their private, personal information publicly revealed) (Megarry, 2017). Even though this kind of gendered, digital violence creates toxic areas for women, women still report finding digital platforms like Twitter a safer and easier space for engaging in feminist activities (Mendes et al., 2018).

The Case and Methodology

As we study digital feminism through the case of Turkey – #ChallengeAccepted and #IstanbulConventionSavesLives – we remember the advice Foust and Hoyt (2018) gave to researchers of social media movements, which include:

> recognizing movements as rhetorical achievements and constitutive forces that cohere to collective identity; placing these movements within their particular cultural, political, and historical contexts; understanding the overlapping networks of mediations that circulate movement messages and expressions; and recognizing the often contradictory role of human agency within the evolution of these movements.
>
> (p. 51)

To this end, we recognize our "blind spots" that emerge from our identities – Berna is from Turkey and has been active in the feminist movement there, while her race and class privileges have allowed her to study for an advanced degree in the US. As a woman who grew up in Turkey, she has been exposed to and witnessed gender-based violence just like other women in her social circle and her country. She took great responsibilities in the process of writing and getting approval from the parliament, the law no. 6284, which is the only legal practice that plays a role in the protection of women against violence in Turkey. She is an active member of the #IstanbulConventionSavesLives movement as well as being the founding member and first president of the We Will Stop Femicide Platform in 2010. Kristin is American, with much privilege around race, class, and education; as a feminist, they are well-schooled through readings but lack linguistic, cultural, and local lived experience around the case study.

To combat our blind spots, we not only foreground Foust and Hoyt (2018) in our analytic approach, but also Khoja-Moolji (2015), which reminds us to use the critical tools the feminist movement provides us with: "a deep engagement with history, understanding the entanglements of the local with the global, and exploring the unequal gendered relations of power that produce violence against women and girls in the first place" (p. 349). Further, we put into practice feminist standpoint epistemology, which is:

> a unique philosophy of knowledge building that challenges us to (1) see and understand the world through the eyes and experiences of oppressed women and (2) apply the vision and knowledge of oppressed women to social activism and social change.
>
> (Brooks, 2007, p. 55)

As we mentioned at the beginning of the chapter, the #Challenge-Accepted and #IstanbulConventionSavesLives movements, started by women in Turkey, continued on different platforms of the digital environment in order to prevent Turkey from withdrawing from the Istanbul Convention and to take measures against violence against women, especially femicide, which has become unbearable within the country. In accordance with the opportunities offered by each platform, women shared images containing their black and white portraits on Instagram and spread the message "I could have been killed, too," while expressing their thoughts in text with the same hashtags on Twitter. Prior to and during this hashtag campaign, feminists had formed a substantial protest movement in the streets throughout Turkey. Our pilot study of the two digital "branches" of the campaign – close reading/textual analysis on Twitter and semi-structured interviews on Instagram – suggested rich findings on Twitter and Instagram. We focus on reporting these findings in the next sections.

Twitter – #IstanbulConventionSavesLives/ #IstanbulSozlesmesi

A variety of hashtags were used on Twitter, often in combination with one another. To best collect and organize our data, we focused on #IstanbulConventionSavesLives (English) and #IstanbulSozlesmesi (Turkey). The hashtags share meaning and context across the two languages, which allowed us to compare our findings across the two to better understand digital/social media affordances and the potential for digital activism in local, international, and global contexts. The English Tweets numbered 3,361 and the Turkish Tweets numbered 22,998, which on its face suggests that the issue of femicide in Turkey and the removal of Turkey from the Istanbul Convention are more important to Turkish speakers than English speakers. It also suggests that digital media affordances of scalability and participation were limited to the Turkish dataset. Together, the hashtags suggested that they were part of an ecosystem in which they interacted with each other, along with other operators within the sociopolitical environment.

In terms of themes, purposes, and goals, we found many similarities between English language and Turkish language tweets. Both #IstanbulConventionSavesLives and #IstanbulSozlesmesi were used to "identify the problematic situation and its attributions, to decipher who or what to blame, and to suggest a solution" (Khazaraee & Novak, 2018, p. 5). In addition to educating or informing others of "what's happening in Turkey," tweets in English and in Turkish emphasized "amplifying the voices" of women/solidarity and conveying that "Turkey is not safe for women" and "women in Turkey are in danger."

While both hashtags were used to share up-to-date statistics on violence against women and femicide in Turkey, Turkish language tweets shared the more specific content of the Istanbul Convention and how these articles could help keep "us" (women) safe in Turkey. Another key difference in content was the Turkish tweets' emphasis on the self-determination of women. The ten "most liked" tweets were focused on this theme, and three of ten included videos containing images from street protests held alongside the hashtag campaign. This illustrates how for women tweeting in Turkish, #IstanbulSozlesmesi was just one tool in their "digital repertoire" (Khazraee & Losey, 2016), along with digital video, street protests, informative digital visuals or "carrds,"[2] among others.

In English, tweets expressed despair (nobody is listening; can you hear us?), along with pleas for help and for people to spread the word. "Spreading the word" was also important in the Turkish tweets, with both English and Turkish tweeters tagging social media and political "influencers" to call global attention to the indiscriminate murder of women in Turkey. We perceived influencers as driving "social solidarity" (Bao et al., 2020) and recognized solidarity as an important theme in both groups of tweets. English language solidarity was in the third-person, while Turkish language solidarity was in the first-person, reflecting a collective identity. Collective identity and solidarity were so important to the Turkish tweets that we heard it as both a diagnosis of the situation: "Birimiz güvende değilse, hiçbirimiz güvende değiliz! (If one of us is not safe, none of us are safe!)" (2021–03–20 T19:06:43); and a solution: "Daha cesur! Daha yürekli! Daha özgür! Mücadeleye devam" ("Braver! More heartily! Freer! Keep fighting...") (2021–03–20 T05:58:03).

In terms of ecosystem, we saw the hashtags as a network of power relations and mediations. The top 200 English tweets, for instance, were dominated by institutions, politicians, human rights groups, and celebrities. We recognized these user accounts as having a natural legitimacy born from their actual and referent power (Bowers et al., 2010) and other forms of social and/or cultural capital. Thirty-three distinct "power" tweeters were identified, including the Council of Europe (@COE), national foreign affairs ministries (@Greece_MFA; @Norway_MFA...), UN-affiliated groups (@UN_News_Centre; @UNWomen...), politicians (@TerryReintke; @mansuryavas06...), and celebrity entertainers (@GayeSuAkyol; @Elif_Shafak), to name a few. For the most part, "power" tweets admonished (blamed) Turkey or the Turkish government for leaving the Istanbul Convention (problem) and called for the convention to be reinstated (solution).

"Power" tweets described Turkey leaving the Istanbul Convention as: appalling; shameful; unbelievable; deplorable; unacceptable; shocking; regrettable; deeply disappointing, a setback, serious step back, and back slide for human rights; disastrous; really, really bad news, catastrophic; inhumane; just terrible; and an absolute disgrace. Given that a woman is murdered almost every day in Turkey, these denouncements fail to capture the sense of fear and danger experienced by women in Turkey.

As we identified the "power" accounts within the English language tweets, we also identified "people" accounts who were users not affiliated with institutions and not imbued with actual or referent power. We observed strong differences, both in terms of content and the tone, between the "power" and "people" tweets. First and foremost, "power" tweets were more likely to be responding to the situation from outside of Turkey *on behalf of* women in Turkey. This positions the support as paternalistic – which is similar to the misogyny that women in Turkey fight against every day. Not surprisingly, the term *misogyny* was used only five times within these 200 most retweeted and liked tweets. The term *patriarchy* appeared only once. Rather than naming misogyny and patriarchy, these "power" tweets struck a tone of "official response" and thus were muted in the strength of their denunciation. @UN_Women, for instance, "urged" the government of Turkey to "continue protecting women," while @JosefBorrellF (the High Representative of EU for Foreign Affairs and Security) expressed "deep regret" toward the Turkish government's decision.

In contrast, "people" tweets, shared by human rights organizations, individual feminists, women, and/or supporters, were more pointed in their diagnosis of the situation. Within these tweets, the hashtag

#KadınCinayetleriPolitiktir ("femicides are political") was included to target misogyny and patriarchy specifically, which feminism maintains are the root cause of women's oppression and endangerment. While the departure from the Istanbul Convention spurred the hashtag movement, this was only the surface for feminists in Turkey. These women have lived everyday under a regime of femicide, which has allowed men to murder women with impunity, and they were quick to assess the problem as such: "77 women have been murdered in the past 78 days. the country is basically a women cemetery at this point" (2021–03–20 T08:20:35).

As mentioned, another contrast between "power" and "people" tweets was the expression of first-person experiences in the "people" tweets. While the English language tweets did not include personal stories from victims of sex-based violence, they did include emotional and poignant testimonies of what it feels like to be a woman in Turkey:

> I don't want to die I'm too young to die please help us please help Turkey Turkey is not safe for women spread our message.
> (2021–03–20 T12:49:03)

> I've never felt so desperate in my life before. We need your help to live. Please don't ignore us.
> (2021–03–20 T10:59:16)

Whether through spreading the message or not ignoring women in Turkey, "people" tweets were much better than the "power" tweets at providing concrete actions people could take to help. While both groups of tweets embraced the language and sentiment of solidarity, only the "people" gave a to-do list: educate yourself; attend the virtual protest; spread the word; use hashtags; sign petitions.

In the Turkish language ecosystem, the role of "power" or institutional tweets was muted, while "people" tweets were amplified. "Power" tweeters were mostly women's rights organizations; so, unlike English tweets, the tone used was appropriate for both the feelings of women and the struggle rather than being dictating, educating, irresponsible, or an outsider looking in. "People" tweets provided more of a first-person perspective than the English language tweets, and unlike the English language tweets, they included tweets in opposition to the Istanbul Convention.

Within the Turkish dataset, we saw a contentious exchange between supporters of Recep Tayyip Erdoğan and the supporters of woman's rights and self-determination. Opposing tweets accounted for almost 10% of Turkish language tweets. Opposition use of the hashtag focused on hostility toward the feminist movement, demonstrations of misogyny, and advocacy for the Islamist, conservative, and authoritarian political view that President Recep Tayyip Erdoğan represents. Erdogan's power was held as absolute and could not be challenged; those who tried were labeled anti-Islam and found themselves in physical danger. Backlash against #IstanbulSozlesmesi was swift, ferocious, and effective. The counter-hashtag #GüleGüleMorHalka (which means "goodbye to the purple circle," referring to the emblem of feminism in Turkey) emerged as a form of "mediated misogyny" (Vickery & Everbach, 2018) that quickly eclipsed #IstanbulSozlesmesi online and encouraged the violent suppression of women in the real world. Online, women and feminists were forced to redirect their efforts and expend valuable resources to protect the hashtag and keep its content loyal to the Istanbul Convention and the anti-violence against women. Offline, protesting women and feminist face riot police and tear gas (Fahim, 2021) and the increasingly empowered ire of men, whose hatred of women has already produced staggering rates of femicide.

Semi-Structured Interviews with Hashtag "Feminists"

Semi-structured interviews were conducted with 26 women aged between 18 and 64, who actively used the hashtags #ChallengeAccepted and #IstanbulConventionSavesLives on Instagram. The economic classes of the interviewed women vary: six of them unemployed/unpaid domestic workers, one of them retired, three of them workers, and 16 of them work in jobs that can be included in the middle and upper class. None of the participants had a history of activism, except for two, which suggests that digital and social media affordances related to hashtag activism increased participation in this campaign and hastened an "uptake" of feminism (Mendes et al., 2019). We were most interested in honoring women's experiences and hearing their perspectives on the purpose and the political context of #ChallengeAccepted, the role of intersectionality, how well the movement reflected the daily lives of women, and the results that followed their individual and collective participation.

Through the interviews, we found that women knew the root causes for the movement – violence against women and femicide – and were quick to provide concrete numbers and statistics. As in the Tweets we studied, interview participants cited the stark number of femicides ("Every year, more than a hundred women, children and transgender people are killed in Turkey") and the alarming rates at which these crimes are increasing ("Nothing else in Turkey is rising this fast"). Informants also expressed the same kind of despair we heard in the "people" tweets – believing that the Istanbul Convention was the only hope for protecting women in Turkey and that as women, they felt abandoned and in danger ("We had only one contract, they terminated it"; "We have no other contract to protect us").

While on-the-ground situation and prospects for women in Turkey were bleak, the women we interviewed were by no means disempowered or defeated. These informants illustrated how women in Turkey are developing various perspectives on the purpose of the movement, which allows them to keep working in the face of insurmountable odds. "Agenda setting" was most important and it was applied in two dimensions: local and international. The idea that women's voices should be raised against the increasing gender-based violence and femicide occupies and inspires the local agenda: "Let them know that we have a voice"; "We have been silent enough, we will not be anymore"; "[If] I, as an educated, conscious woman, stay silent, how can other women have a voice and be heard?"

In addition to local imperatives, our informants reported growing pressure to focus on an international agenda oriented around the demand for solutions and to help draw attention to the situation in Turkey. We could hear the frustration when our informants said, "They don't listen to us, maybe if they are disgraced to the world, it will have an impact"; and "Our aim was to bring the issue to the international platform and explain that we could not find a solution here." In this way, we see how distinctions between private and public, which are made possible through the affordances of social media, not only nurture agency for these women (Papacharissi, 2015), but also transform the personal (or in this case "local") into the political (Hanisch, 1969).

Whether local or international, the most common purpose of these women's individual participation was to create a solidarity network: "I wanted the women around me to know that they are not alone"; "It is purely for solidarity"; "We stand by each other"; "We will be strong if we are together"; "This is a solidarity movement"; "My biggest expectation was for women to strengthen their power and to feel that we were not alone."

In addition to creating a solidarity network, our respondents reported other reasons for participating in the hashtag activism. One stated that the gains to be made for women, whom she described as a disadvantaged group, would be a source of hope for the children, lesbian, gay, bisexual, transgender, and intersex (LGBTI) community and animals, whom she also defined as disadvantaged. Another referenced Pınar Gültekin's (the woman whose murder triggered the movement) Kurdish identity as having a profound effect on how she responded to the femicide. This respondent hoped that the overwhelming support for this murdered woman, regardless of her racial identity, might change everyone's perspective on Kurdish people in Turkey who are marginalized as second-class citizens or worse, erased from sociocultural institutions altogether (Bakan & Saluk, 2020).

Another participant echoed this appreciation diversity and inclusion and stated that "I am frankly pleased to be able to meet women who I think have different values and views, [and still share] the common point of 'women.'" These points are important to emphasize, because both Turkey and feminism have struggled around intersectionality and have failed to recognize how gender, race, and class interact and overlap and inform systems of privilege and oppression. It was noted that 12 of our informants (almost half of our sample) used the statement "Turkish woman," which fails to recognize Kurdish, Armenian, and Arab women within the population. Similarly, we observed a lack of emphasis on class identity among our informants, thus further suggesting weakness within the intersectional structure of the movement.

In assessing potential outcomes and "success" of the movement, only two of our informants thought that their actions could prevent the withdrawal of the Istanbul Convention. This means that 92% of our sample engaged in hashtag feminism they knew would not produce any real-world result. Our informants expressed little belief that social power could bring any administrative change in Turkey ("Hundreds of thousands of people protested in Gezi Park for days, the result was nothing"), noting that the oppressive regime does not take public opinion into account ("They are trying to silence everyone who oppose them") and in their cases does not value women's lives ("They don't care if we die, why should they protect us?"). One participant strikingly captured the collective attitude around the effectiveness of online activism when she said: "I do not think that such campaigns will work. I even shared my photo in color."

Like Mendes et al. (2019), the effects of digital feminism on the daily lives of women were the most encouraging of our findings. In this respect, almost all the participants stated that they felt the movement had positive effects in their lives. First, the women expressed being happy that they had the courage to speak up and to create an agenda and that their participation made them feel empowered: "I have shown what I stand for"; "What I felt was the strength and pride of the unity of women all over the world"; "We, who have been silent for so long with fear, are now more courageous. I think that was the biggest effect."

Through our informants, we were reminded that the informative aspect of the campaign also carries weight and that women were motivated around informational needs. Sometimes the participating women themselves obtain information and learn something from the movement ("I learned the content of the articles of the Istanbul Convention"; "I was not aware of the Convention and learned it through the campaign"; "I read all the articles and realized that if they were implemented, Pınar and the other women we have lost would be with us today"). Other times, the women joined the movement to post informative content to teach and educate others ("People do not know the content of the contract, or they know it wrong. Therefore, they are against it"; "I thought maybe someone would open and read the contract"; "I shared all the information I could find. I sent it to all WhatsApp groups, even to our business group").

The interviews brought the affordance of digital feminism to allow for mass participation to the forefront. Fourteen of the participants stated that they were part of a feminist movement for the first time with this campaign and that their efforts included promoting the movement and feminism to their social circles. In this way, the public's uptake of feminism increased, as feminist's uptake of digital media increased (Mendes et al., 2019). Even though our sample noted the affordance of "ease" in doing digital hashtag feminism, more than half also reported experiencing misogyny after their participation ("They created a counter-hashtag and tried to defame our campaign"; "It was a weird experience for me because I got backlash from people close to me not only on social media but also in real life"; "There were even people who texted swearwords in my DM box"; "Sure, we had a problem with my boyfriend. Because he thought I disgraced him").

Although only two of the interviewed women did not use sociopolitical concepts such as "patriarchy" and "sexism" that point to the structural problem when expressing their views, we found the same concepts expressed indirectly through their use of the terms "regime," "system," and "government." That the informants linked these supposedly benign terms so completely with "patriarchy," "sexism," and "structural oppression" that they could be used interchangeably is a chilling reminder of how infected our systems and institutions are with these ills.

Conclusion

Regardless of where one falls in the debate over the efficacy of digital media technologies in democratic struggles for change, it is clear that the digital environment has had a transformative effect on feminism.

In the case of Turkey and around the globe, feminists have developed a "digital repertoire" (Khazraee & Losey, 2016) that accompanies traditional methods of struggle to form a hybrid ecology (Treré, 2018) and effectively mobilizes and grows the movement. Several of our interview respondents reported engaging in feminism for the first time through the #IstanbulSozlesmesi campaign, proving that as feminists take up digital media technologies, more people take up feminism (Mendes et al., 2019).

This uptake of feminism confirms that the digital media affordance that allows for mass participation was at work locally in Turkey. Globally, however, mass participation failed to materialize. The disparity in the number of tweets – 22,998 in Turkish, 3,361 in English – suggests that the "ease" in participating in the hashtag activism was concentrated in Turkey, affecting the outcomes of the movement. Mass participation fuels local and international agenda setting and thus impacts the amount of pressure put on decision-makers for the desired gain. Further, it encourages women to speak up, oppose, and realize feminist praxis by bringing the private sphere into the public sphere through the sharing of their individual experiences. The ecosystem of the hashtags, the rise of mediated misogyny, and the failure to address intersectionality within feminism in Turkey all posed challenges to mass participation.

The network of power and mediation that structured tweets, especially in English, discouraged mass participation by heightening the distance between the tweeter, the problem of violence against women/femicide in Turkey, and the global audience for the tweet. Softly worded denouncements by institutional "power" tweeters centered the Istanbul Convention (a benign document to global audiences) rather than femicide statistics in a way that did not provide for "connectivity" across audiences (Bennett & Segerberg, 2013).

While official, institutional "power" tweeters were downplaying the systemic violence against women in Turkey via language, Turkish language tweets were threatening women through the language of misogyny. Undeniably, digital affordances that help make digital activism "easy" are also easily co-opted by dark forces. In the hybrid ecology provided by traditional and digital media, misogyny sometimes emerges as mediated (as seen in #GüleGüleMorHalka), sometimes through physical danger (threatening messages), and sometimes through discursive/tonal framing that dismisses the brutal reality of the situation (international "power" tweets). Regardless of form, misogyny puts up a strong barrier to participation as women must choose between raising their voice and protecting their lives.

Some women, however, are not given a choice. We were especially conscious of intersectionality, because in Turkey women are shut out of digital and social media due to varying economic, religious, and class oppression reasons. Both in the tweets we analyzed and in our interview responses, we heard nothing of marginalized groups. At best, tweeters referred to "women in Turkey," and at worst, "Turkish women," which suggests that all women in Turkey are Turkish, when they are not. These erased women are also exposed to oppression of systems of power and neoliberalism and patriarchy in multiple layers are indispensable components of women's struggle.

Despite all the impositions of neoliberalism and the individualism it brings, it is necessary to appreciate the solidarity network created by digital feminism. In addition, in countries like Turkey where many democratic gains have been lost, street struggles are prevented by oppressive and authoritarian regimes, and therefore society's belief in making change has decreased. It is very valuable to catch the light of hope that our participants expressed: "if not today, then tomorrow." This tenacity of women, expressed so poignantly in the Turkish language tweets and by our interview respondents, underscores the nuanced expectations and outcomes participants pull from their hashtag activism. Our interviewees confessed that they had little or no hope that their participation would change the outcome of the Istanbul Convention. Still, they answered each other's calls to be "Braver! More heartily! Freer!" (2021–03–20 T05:58:03). They kept fighting and walked away with a different kind of social change – "We, who have been silent for so long with fear, are now more courageous. I think that was the biggest effect."

Notes

1 The Istanbul Convention is more formally known as the Council of Europe Convention on preventing and combating violence against women and domestic violence.
2 A one-page site users can produce for free at https://carrd.co/ and share through multiple digital platforms.

References

Alsahi, H. (2018). The Twitter Campaign to end the male guardianship system in Saudi Arabia. *Journal of Arabian Studies*, 8(2), 298–318.
Amnesty International Australia. (2020). Using digital tools for Activism Level 2: Fundamental activist skills [Brochure]. Amnesty International. https://www.amnesty.org.au/wp-content/uploads/2020/05/208-using-digital-tools-for-activism.pdf

Bakan, R., & Saluk, S. (2020). *Challenge accepted? Systemic erasures in femicide narratives from Turkey.* Jadalliya. https://www.jadaliyya.com/Details/41561/Challenge-Accepted-Systematic-Erasures-in-Femicide-Narratives-from-Turkey-41561

Banet-Weiser, S. (2018). *Empowered: Popular feminism and popular misogyny.* Duke University Press.

Banet-Weiser, S. (2019). Popular feminism and popular misogyny. In Nelson Ribeiro and Barbie Zelizer (Eds), *Media and populism,* 1st Lisbon Winter School for the Study of Communication (pp. 68–80). Research Center for Communication & Culture: Lisbon.

Banet-Weiser, S., Gill, R., & Rottenberg, C. (2020). Postfeminism, popular feminism and neoliberal feminism? Sarah Banet-Weiser, Rosalind Gill and Catherine Rottenberg in conversation. *Feminist Theory, 21*(1), 3–24.

Bao, H., Cao, B., Xiong, Y., & Tang, W. (2020). Digital media's role in the COVID-19 pandemic. *JMIR mHealth and uHealth, 8*(9), e20156.

Baumgardner, J. (2011). *F'em!: Goo goo, gaga, and some thoughts on balls.* Seal Press.

Bennett, W. L., & Segerberg, A. (2013). *The logic of connective action: Digital media and the personalization of contentious politics.* Cambridge University Press.

Bennett, W. L., & Segerberg, A. (2015). Communication in movements. In D. Della Porta, & M. Diani (Eds.), *The Oxford handbook of social movements* (pp. 367–382). Oxford University Press.

Bowers, J. W., Ochs, D. J., Jensen, R. J., & Schulz, D. P. (2010). *The rhetoric of agitation and control (Third edition).* Waveland Press.

Brooks, A. (2007). Feminist standpoint epistemology: Building knowledge and empowerment through women's lived experience. In S. N. Hesse-Biber, & P. L. Leavy (Eds.), *Feminist research practice: A primer* (pp. 53–82). Sage Publishing.

Cammaerts, B. (2015). Technologies of self-mediation: Affordances and constraints of social media for protest movements. In A. Vestergaard, & J. Uldam (Eds.), *Civic engagement and social media* (pp. 87–110). Palgrave Macmillan.

Castells, M. (2012) *Networks of outrage and hope: Social movements in the internet age.* Polity.

Cho, A. (2018). Default publicness: Queer youth of color, social media, and being outed by the machine. *New Media & Society, 20*(9), 3183–3200. https://doi.org/10.1177/1461444817744784

Fahim, K. (2021, July 1). *Women protest in Turkey after government withdraws from treaty combating gender-based violence.* The Washington Post. https://www.washingtonpost.com/world/istanbul-convention-turkey-erdogan-protests-women-domestic-violence/2021/07/01/3cd93ac8-daa1-11eb-8c87-ad6f27918c78_story.html

Foust, C. R., & Hoyt, K. D. (2018). Social movement 2.0: Integrating and assessing scholarship on social media and movement. *Review of Communication, 18*(1), 37–55.

Fox, K., & Diehm, J. (2017). # MeToo's global moment: The anatomy of a viral campaign. *CNN*, November, 9.

Flesher Fominaya, C., & Gillan, K. (2017). Navigating the technology-media-movements complex. *Social Movement Studies, 16*(4), 383–402.

Gibbs, M., Meese, J., Arnold, M., Nansen, B., & Carter, M. (2015). # Funeral and Instagram: Death, social media, and platform vernacular. *Information, Communication & Society, 18*(3), 255–268.

Hanisch, C. (1969). The personal is political. Retrieved July 31, 2021, from http://www.carolhanisch.org/CHwritings/PIP.html

Herman, Edward S., & Chomsky, N. (1988). *Manufacturing consent: The political economy of the mass media.* Pantheon.

hooks, b. (2000). *Feminism is for everybody: Passionate politics.* Pluto Press.

Iosifidis, P., & Wheeler, M. (2015). The public sphere and network democracy: Social movements and political change?. *Global Media Journal, 13*(25), 1–17.

Kavada, A. (2016). Social movements and political agency in the digital age: A communication approach. *Media and Communication, 4*(4), 8–12.

Khazraee, E., & Losey, J. (2016). Evolving repertoires: Digital media use in contentious politics. *Communication and the Public, 1*(1), 39–55.

Khazraee, E., & Novak, A. N. (2018). Digitally mediated protest: Social media affordances for collective identity construction. *Social Media+ Society, 4*(1), 2056305118765740.

Khoja-Moolji, S. (2015). Becoming an "intimate publics": Exploring the affective intensities of hashtag feminism. *Feminist Media Studies, 15*(2), 347–350.

Kucukgocmen, A., & Usta, B. (2021). Around 1,000 women gather in Istanbul to protest against femicides. *Reuters*. Retrieved July 31, 2021, from https://www.reuters.com/article/us-womens-day-turkey/around-1000-women-gather-in-istanbul-to-protest-against-femicides-idUSKBN2B02BX

Lekach, S. (2017, October 19). #MeToo hashtag has spread to #YoTambien, #أنا_كمان, #QuellaVoltaChe. *Mashable*. Retrieved July 31, 2021, from https://mashable.com/article/me-too-global-spread

Lim, M. (2018). Roots, routes, and routers: Communications and media of contemporary social movements. *Journalism & Communication Monographs, 20*(2), 92–136.

Martin, G. (2015). *Understanding social movements.* Routledge.

Megarry, J. (2017). Why# metoo is an impoverished form of feminist activism, unlikely to spark social change. *The Conversation*. Retrieved July 31, 2021, from https://theconversation.com/why-metoo-is-an-impoverished-form-of-feminist-activism-unlikely-to-spark-social-change-86455

Mendes, K., Ringrose, J., & Keller, J. (2018). # MeToo and the promise and pitfalls of challenging rape culture through digital feminist activism. *European Journal of Women's Studies, 25*(2), 236–246.

Mendes, K., Ringrose, J., & Keller, J. (2019). *Digital feminist activism: Girls and women fight back against rape culture.* Oxford University Press.

Meyer, M. D., & Bray, C. W. (2013). Emerging adult usage of social networks as sites of activism: A critical examination of the TOMS and TWLOHA movements. *Ohio Communication Journal, 51*(October), 53–77.

Munro, E. (2013). Feminism: A fourth wave? *Political Insight*, *4*(2), 22–25.

Papacharissi, Z. (2015). *Affective publics: Sentiment, technology, and politics.* Oxford University Press.

Schradie, J. A. (2014). *This is (Not) What Democracy Looks Like: How Ideology, Hierarchy, and Inequality Shape Digital Activism* (Doctoral dissertation, UC Berkeley).

Shapshak, T. (2016). *WhatsApp shut down in Zimbabwe during protests – Following Burundi, DRC, Uganda.* Forbes. https://www.forbes.com/sites/tobyshapshak/2016/07/06/whatsapp-shut-down-in-zimbabwe-during-protests-following-burundi-drc-uganda/?sh=686285afd6e4

Şimşek, B. (2019). *Why can't femicide be prevented?.* BBCNews. https://www.bbc.com/turkce/haberler-turkiye-49492456

Treem, J. W., & Leonardi, P. M. (2013). Social media use in organizations: Exploring the affordances of visibility, editability, persistence, and association. *Annals of the International Communication Association*, *36*(1), 143–189.

Treré, E. (2018). *Hybrid media activism: Ecologies, imaginaries, algorithms.* Routledge.

Vickery, J. R., & Everbach, T. (Eds.). (2018). *Mediating misogyny: Gender, technology, and harassment.* Springer.

Warfield, K. (2016). Making the cut: An agential realist examination of selfies and touch. *Social Media+ Society*, *2*(2), 1–10. 2056305116641706.

Waisbord, S. (2011). Can NGOs change the news?. *International Journal of Communication*, *5*, 24.

What's App (2021). Retrieved July 31, 2021, from https://www.whatsapp.com/

Yilmaz, S. R. (2017). The role of social media activism in new social movements: Opportunities and limitations. *International Journal of Social Inquiry*, *10*(1), 141–164.

5 Politics of Artificial Intelligence Adoption

Unpacking the Regime Type Debate

H. Akın Ünver and Arhan S. Ertan

Introduction

Over the last decade, the diffusion and adoption of artificial intelligence (A.I.) and its related technologies across the world became a new flashpoint of international competition. Although developed Western nations were initially better positioned to seize primacy in this new technological domain due to their stronger industrial base, the rapid advance and export strategies of Chinese high-tech industries have facilitated the diffusion of A.I. into countries with relatively less developed industrial and scientific foundations such as Ethiopia, Myanmar, and Zimbabwe. Such medium-cost, medium-capability A.I. exports so far included speech and face recognition, personal data push services, interactive interface technologies, data transmission infrastructure, and hardware devices required to transfer and process such data (Gravett, 2020). Often, these individual software and hardware bundles are exported under 'smart/ safe city' or 'smart policing' marketing strategies, although the fundamental 'detection-processing-prediction' task chain is near-identical and redeployable across various projects (Roberts et al., 2021).

Chinese exports render automation at scale more affordable for developing countries by trading readily deployable A.I. tools cheaper, and in most cases, assist automation efforts of technologically less developed countries by reducing their dependence on trained human capital. This cost-effective Chinese A.I. export doctrine helps importer countries streamline decisions without having to train and employ armies of highly skilled programmers or engineers. While these countries cannot compete with more advanced and indigenously developed A.I. technologies of the US, EU, or Japan, they gain a clear advantage over their regional rivals that cannot afford Western A.I. technologies, yet also don't import from China due to their US alliance commitments (Aly, 2020). Over time, developing nations that embargo

DOI: 10.4324/9781003173427-5

Chinese A.I. exports due to their alliance commitments to the US or the EU or due to ethical concerns about Chinese A.I. lose their competing power against other rivals that are bound by neither and look to Beijing for high-tech imports. Therein lies the Chinese comparative advantage in A.I. exports and the core of the global competition for technological influence between the US and China: Chinese strategy is as much about controlling global cost-effective A.I. demand and defining the mainstream market as it is about competing with the US.

As the technique and skillset ecosystem of A.I. expands, it becomes a general purpose technology (GPT). The more the A.I. ecosystem grows and its constituent technologies become more complicated, what specifically such technologies entail becomes subject to greater debate. While the general consensus of A.I. definition still focuses on human-like behavior or decisions from machines, the scale and accuracy at which such expressions manifest form the basis of the international competition over algorithms, talent, and hardware that render these possible (Horowitz, 2018). In simpler terms, 'A.I. exports' are generally defined as hardware, algorithm and software units, bundles, and combinations that are intended to automate a large array of tasks that are repetitive in nature, but require human-like vision, decisions, and assessment procedures (Greitens, 2020; Helm et al., 2020). These mostly relate, but aren't exclusive to, a combination of advances in machine learning, robotic and vehicular autonomy, large-scale complex statistics, human-machine interaction, computer vision/language/agents, and neural networks. As a developing ecosystem of technologies, what specifically A.I. can do at the strategic level is still being hypothesized at the military, social, economic, healthcare, and educational domains with some applied convergence (Wang, 2019). At the very least, grasping the true impact of A.I. on broader global economic and social systems will take at least another decade, given how long it took for previous GPTs to be absorbed into their zeitgeist (Petralia, 2021). With such a lack of generally accepted parameters over what specifically 'A.I. technologies' entail and are expected to do, countries find it increasingly difficult to assess whether their national A.I. strategies are successful or how to strategize wielding A.I. in trade, defense, and diplomacy. This is why, while most countries realize that investing in A.I. is important, they are largely divided over how much they should invest in it (or which specific component) and which leading nations to cooperate with to maximize the chances of a successful A.I. adoption (Meltzer & Kerry, 2021).

Amidst this uncertainty, the US and China grew locked into a competition over global A.I. dominance, both trying to maximize their respective capacities and exporting their own products to the world. Both countries prioritize capitalizing on the rapid growth in computing capacity, producing and processing increasingly bigger datasets, develop newer and more sophisticated algorithms and statistical methods to increase the quality of their predictions, and creating an investment ecosystem that can financially sustain these advances over the long term. Additionally, both countries seek to leverage A.I. to build and maintain new alliance and partnership patterns that can bolster their international standing and export dominance. Quite often, this political feud spills over into complementary technologies such as 5G cellular networks, quantum computing, semiconductors, and autonomous vehicles, broadening the trenches of the competition over emerging technologies, and rendering this competition a truly global one with system-level balance of power repercussions (Horowitz et al., 2018).

Politics of Artificial Intelligence: The Regime Type Debate

In the last few years, scholarship on how countries adopt and employ A.I. tools and techniques grew significantly. Amidst this debate, major fields of inquiry sought to explain the spread of such technologies from a diverse array of theories such as development and growth, organizational adaptation, welfare and inequality, politics, and international competition (Alsheibani et al., 2018; Webster & Ivanov, 2020; Weber & Schütte, 2019; Zerfass et al., 2020). Within the political science and international relations scholarship, researchers have largely focused on whether governance and political systems affect how countries adopt new technologies. In other words: does regime type (whether a country is democratic or authoritarian) affect whether or how countries adopt artificial intelligence (Levy, 2018; Malmborg & Trondal, 2021; Schiff et al., 2021; Unver, 2018)? As promising extensions of this research question, further inquiries emerged into whether automation at scale will be more conducive to democracy or authoritarianism or whether unemployment and labor shifts generated by mass automation will reinforce autocratic tendencies of governments (Feldstein, 2019a; Frank et al., 2019; Zeng, 2020).

Since technology adoption is a multilayered process that is determined at the intersection of a nation's government, citizens, and corporations, the political system under which these actors operate determines the scope and depth of such adoption (Evans, 1995). In the case of A.I., technology companies that drive high-tech adoption rely on sound regulatory environment, uninterrupted and predictable funding streams, and an investment environment that is conducive for international collaborations and partnerships (Milner, 2006). In line with the adoption patterns of other digital technologies, when a political system is free enough to secure a rapid development of private technological enterprise and enable citizens and companies to use new products produced by such companies unhindered, one can expect democratic countries to lead in A.I (Corrales & Westhoff, 2006).

Governments have a number of incentives in providing a conducive environment for A.I. technology adoption. Automation at scale renders a wide array of tasks in national defense, industrial production, banking/finance, and communication faster at higher volumes and increasingly more accurate (Diamond, 2010; Viscusi et al., 2020). A robust A.I. infrastructure itself positions nations better to adopt rapidly developing advanced technologies and thereby increase the competitiveness of those countries' defense, commerce, industry, and trade sectors (Haner & Garcia, 2019). To that end, willingness to adopt and develop advanced A.I. know-how generates global interest irrespective of regime types.

Yet, there have been studies that emphasize particular characteristics of democracies to distinctly enable a faster and more robust adoption of newer technologies. According to this stream, freer political systems and less centralized economic systems are better positioned to create scientific and industrial ecosystems that can enable better adoption of digital technologies (Kimber, 1991; Leslie et al., 2021; Nemitz, 2018; Wright, 2020). Corrales and Westhoff (2006), for example, demonstrate that democracies, on average, adopted the Internet faster and with greater nationwide penetration compared to authoritarian governments. Milner (2006), however, posits that democracies are not inherently more conducive to the adoption of new technologies, but elite preferences in autocracies define whether that country will adopt an emerging technology. This line of argumentation suggests that if authoritarian leaders believe a new technology will reinforce their rule, they will create conducive funding and investment environment to facilitate new technology adoption. For example, an authoritarian country may restrict the adoption and spread of the Internet and social media due to their regime-weakening effects, but actively facilitate and encourage the development of an A.I. industry due to their defense and surveillance implications. In Acemoglu and Robinson's (2000, 126–127) words: 'agents who have political power and fear losing it who will have incentives to block technological progress'.

Yet, Stier (2015) introduces a temporal argument in his cross-sectional study, empirically demonstrating that after 2013, there are no clear differences in Internet adoption between democracies and authoritarian countries, as the latter have caught up rapidly once they learned how to manage and control digital communication outlets (Druzin & Gordon, 2018; Rød & Weidmann, 2015). In that vein, technology adoption can also be viewed as a matter of regime survival, whereby active elite preferences matter more than passive regime type effects. Once such technologies demonstrably reduce costs of surveillance and control, they trigger a very different form of technology diffusion across hybrid and authoritarian regimes that cannot be explained by the democratic technology diffusion literature (Choi & Jee, 2021). Kania's (2021) exploration of Chinese People's Liberation Army doctrine on artificial intelligence is particularly important in this sense, as it is expected to influence defense doctrines of other developing nations that are likely to import A.I. components heavily from China. In her work, Kania demonstrates how China has situated its armed forces and revisionist territorial claims in the South China Sea as the main engine of its broader A.I. efforts, outlining that authoritarian countries with similar revisionist claims may find it more desirable to acquire advanced technologies from China rather than Western nations.

But why would A.I. adoption patterns flow across similar regime types? One line of scholarship explores whether A.I. is a distinctly liberal or illiberal technology. Wright (2020), for example, focuses on the surveillance-enhancing aspects of A.I. to posit that such technologies, under authoritarian hands, will reinforce further repression and will embolden other authoritarian countries to adopt A.I. tools that make it easier to engage in large-scale spying on citizens. To prevent such a scenario, he emphasizes the role of civil society and democratic institutions to bolster international A.I. governance norms to facilitate technology diffusion among democratic nations, thereby rendering authoritarian adoption of A.I. undesirable for developing nations. Lamensch (2021) posits a similar argument, demonstrating how A.I. in particular and digital technologies in general are more conducive for authoritarian tendencies rather than liberal ones by reducing the costs of large-scale surveillance. That said, she underlines the fact that a broad range of A.I. tools used by authoritarian regimes are developed and exported by democracies themselves, blurring the lines between various regime types and how much they contribute to global authoritarianism.

Polyakova and Meserole (2019), however, argue that it is no longer democracies alone that are exporting A.I. technologies to authoritarian countries, but Chinese and Russian low-cost options are increasingly clawing back market share from Western exports, creating distinct regime type cleavages in technological trade patterns. They argue in favor of stronger export controls to minimize the transfer of surveillance and A.I.-related technologies from democracies into authoritarian regimes and opt for targeted sanctions on critical technologies in more extreme cases. Similarly, by deploying a large dataset of A.I. adoption trends, Feldstein (2019a) outlines three main pathways for how A.I. can reinforce illiberalism: mass surveillance that disables popular movements and protests, localized surveillance to suppress dissent in protest-prone regions, and deploying organized large-scale disinformation to delegitimize the political opposition. He posits that while these techniques are problematic enough under Chinese control, exporting such technologies to bolster autocracies across the world reduces developing countries' reliance on Western A.I. exports, thereby bypassing the need to adopt democratic norms and practices as prerequisites to access advanced technologies.

As an increasing number of democratic regimes began importing A.I. tools from China, the regime type became particularly salient from an international alliances point of view – especially on whether A.I. trading patterns will generate new alliance formations such as hybrid ones that include a mixture of regime types. Since post-World War II and post-Cold War world orders are built on institutionalizing cooperation among democracies and forming a unified bloc against authoritarian countries, A.I.-related conflict and cooperation patterns are generally expected to follow a similar course. Franke (2021), for example, situates the EU firmly within the US-led A.I. alliance system, arguing that regime type and democratic norms will remain as the fundamental conditions for cooperation and partnership patterns in the next decade. Additionally, she prescribes that to attain primacy in the new A.I. competition, the EU would have to prioritize bolstering the private sector and technology startups rather than state-led initiatives by individual member states. Horowitz (2018) argues that international alliance and balance of power shifts will largely be dictated by whichever country leads in the scientific and military advances in A.I. He warns that a US-led A.I. supremacy is by no means guaranteed, and if the current trend in deep learning research continues, it might be likelier for China to create a new partnership regime – one that may even include most European countries – based on its lower-cost high technology exports.

As outlined in Johnson (2019), an increasing number of countries view A.I. as a strategic investment priority and view any progress in this field as a national security goal. As a testament to A.I.'s growing importance, while there were only three countries with national A.I. strategies in 2016, as of 2021, there are more than 60. In one of the most comprehensive of such analyses, Fatima et al. (2020) find great discrepancies over how countries discursively construct A.I. in their national strategy documents. They conclude that democratic countries with a lower technology base are more likely to emphasize ethical dimensions of A.I. in their national strategy documents compared to democratic or authoritarian/hybrid regimes with a stronger technology base. Yet, even countries with no national strategy documents are involved in strategic A.I. trade. Campbell (2008) focused on China's exports to sub-Saharan African countries underlining that Beijing was reinforcing existing illiberal tendencies of countries by rendering repression easier. Zeng (2020) advances this argument further, positing that the fundamental Chinese A.I. strategy is to bolster states against societies and thereby attract surveillance-oriented developing countries into Chinese technology exports orbit.

From this survey, we arrive at the following hypotheses:

H1: Authoritarian regimes are more likely to choose Chinese A.I. exports
H2: Less developed and poorer countries are more likely to choose Chinese A.I. exports
H3: Countries that have existing strong trade relations with China are more likely to acquire A.I. technologies from them
H4: Authoritarian countries are more likely to acquire surveillance and repression-related A.I. technologies
H5: Belt and Road Initiative (BRI) countries are more likely to acquire Chinese A.I. exports

Data Sources and Methodology

In order to test these hypotheses, we combined two of the most comprehensive datasets that dissect A.I. trade and adoption patterns across the world. The first of these datasets is the Artificial Intelligence Index[1] published by Stanford University's Human-Centered Artificial Intelligence (HAI), which logs A.I. adoption trends across seven categories: research and development, technical performance, economy, A.I. education, ethical challenges of A.I., diversity in A.I., and A.I. policy and national strategy. These categories are then merged into the 'Global A.I. Vibrancy Tool', which measures countries' A.I.-related progress across 22 indicators, including conference papers, journal citations, patents, funded companies, and skill penetration. The second dataset we use is the A.I. Global Surveillance (AIGS) Index, published by Carnegie Endowment, which combines regime type scores, military expenditures, major tech firms in operation, and the type of A.I. technology used by 73 countries (Feldstein, 2019b). The dataset also contains information whether China, US, or Japan is actively involved in those countries' A.I. ecosystems. AIGS also uses Freedom House weighted average country scores, Economist Intelligence Unit (EIU) Democracy Index 2018 and V-Dem's Electoral Democracy Index, to measure regime type as well as Stockholm International Peace Research Institute's (SIPRI's) military expenditure dataset to measure budget and spending-related figures. BRI country information comes from Kliman and Grace (2018), and Chinese overseas direct investment figures are compiled from EIU. Our trade (export-import) data comes from World Bank's World Integrated Trade Solution (WITS) dataset.[2]

In order to analyze our hypotheses, we estimate models in the following linear form:

$$y_i = \alpha + \beta_z z_i + \beta_x x_i + \epsilon_i$$

where y is one of our dependent variables, z and x are the vectors of the explanatory and control variables in our dataset respectively, and ε is the random error term. As for the estimation method, we have utilized the multinomial logit since our dependent variable has more than two mutually exclusive and exhaustive categories which are nominal in nature and do not have a meaningful sequential order. Multinomial logit models are a direct generalization of the ordinary two-outcome (binary) logit models and are used to estimate relationships between an ordinal (categorical or ordered) dependent variable and a set of independent variables. In multinomial logit, an underlying score is estimated as a linear function of the independent variables and a set of cut-points and the error term is assumed to be logistically distributed. Parameter estimation is performed through an iterative maximum likelihood algorithm (Hausman & McFadden, 1984; Small & Hsiao, 1985).

Findings

Our results demonstrate a more nuanced picture with regard to the extent regime type (Hypothesis-1) influences whether countries prefer American or Chinese A.I. exports. Primarily, we offer a more inequality- and development-oriented explanation (i.e., gross domestic product [GDP] differences between countries and whether a country is industrialized and has an existing strong technological base) rather than a regime type explanation (whether a country is democratic or authoritarian) over states' A.I.-related acquisition choices.

With regard to our Hypothesis-2, countries with a greater number of existing A.I. firms tend to rely on both American and Chinese A.I. investments, whereas countries with slightly fewer number of A.I. firms rely predominantly on the US. However, countries that have few or no

A.I. firms import mainly from China (see: Figure 5.1 and Table 5.1). This is an interesting finding, since the number of existing firms in a country and existing technological base push that technology ecosystem towards both the US and China rather than just the US alone. This means that top performer countries in A.I. diversify their technology imports between two technology superpowers and do not rely wholly on the US alone. However, countries with higher A.I. investment budgets prefer US A.I. exports, whereas countries with lower A.I. investment budgets import heavily from China, producing a clear inequality hypothesis (see Figure 5.2). Therefore, greater existing technological base, if measured by the number of existing A.I. firms, pushes countries to diversify into US and Chinese exports. However, if existing technological base is measured by countries' investment budgets, then such countries tend to rely primarily on the US.

As far as Hypothesis-3 is concerned, existing trade relations are strong determinants of countries' A.I. import choices. Countries where China covers a larger portion of imports than the US tend to import A.I. technologies from China at a significant rate (see: Figure 5.4 and Table 5.1). Moreover, countries that have increasingly become more dependent on trade with China in the last 20 years (growth of imports from China versus from the US between 2000 and 2019), strongly prefer

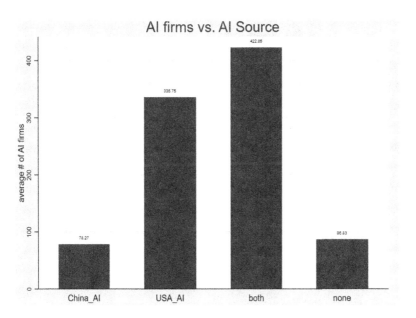

Figure 5.1 Chinese versus US A.I. import preference in sample countries according to the median number of existing AI firms.

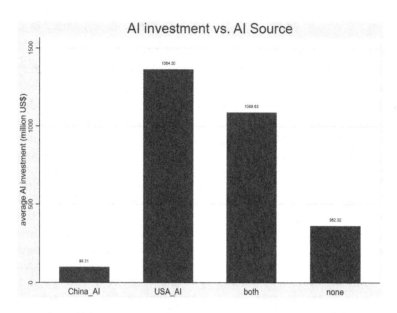

Figure 5.2 Chinese versus US A.I. import preference in sample countries according to the median size of existing AI investment.

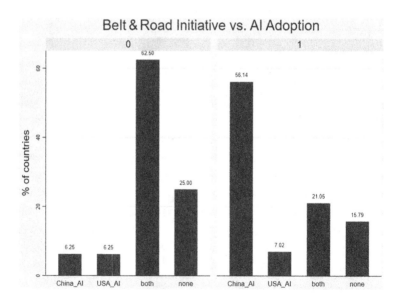

Figure 5.3 Chinese versus US A.I. import preference in sample countries by Belt & Road Initiative participation.

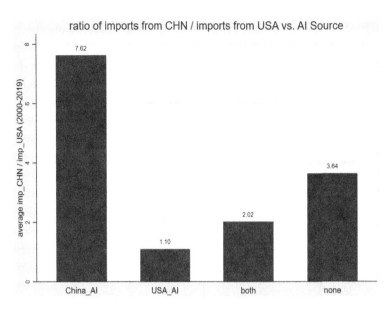

Figure 5.4 Chinese versus US A.I. import preference in sample countries by ratio of imports from China to from USA.

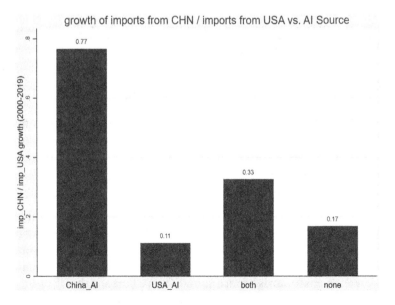

Figure 5.5 Chinese versus US A.I. import preference in sample countries by the ratio of import growth from China.

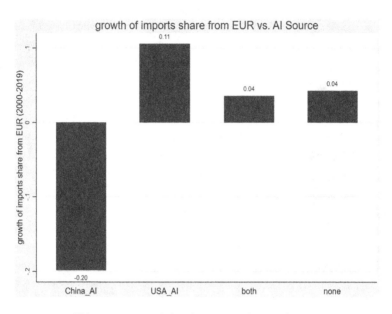

Figure 5.6 Chinese versus US A.I. import preference in sample countries by the ratio of import growth from the EU.

Chinese A.I. exports to American ones (see: Figure 5.5 and Table 5.1). This kind of clear difference doesn't appear in countries where the EU is a dominant trade partner; in countries where the EU is the largest trading partner, preference for A.I. technology from China, US, or both show similar results (suggesting EU-origin A.I. export preferences). Yet, in countries where trade with the EU has grown stronger over the last 20 years, preference for Chinese A.I. imports is significantly lower (see: Figure 5.6). This reinforces the hypothesis that Chinese A.I. exports fill the gap in countries where both American and European trade have dwindled, and thereby situate China as an alternative source of development funds in countries that cannot access any Western sources.

Exploring Hypothesis-5 yields additional insights that weaken the regime-type argument. Being a 'Belt and Road Initiative country' (BRI Group) is a strong indicator of whether a country imports such infrastructure from China (see: Figure 5.3). However, even in non-BRI countries, preference is towards importing both from China and the US rather than heavily or solely from the US. This means that non-BRI countries choose both Chinese and American A.I. exports rather than US-made alone. Therefore, although BRI is a strong anchor that ties a wide range of countries to China's global efforts, Chinese A.I. presence is strong in countries that aren't within the BRI framework. This somewhat refutes arguments of a 'new A.I. Cold War' between the US and China (Garcia, 2021), as in terms of global market dominance, China is the leading supplier of A.I. technologies to a broader and more numerous range of countries. In most countries the US export to, American A.I. firms have to compete with their Chinese counterparts.

As for our Hypothesis-1 and Hypothesis-4, with regard to 'authoritarian A.I. tools' such as facial recognition and surveillance exports, we see no clear difference between the US or Chinese-origin import preferences: facial recognition and related technologies are imported from either/both countries in a comparable fashion, weakening the US-led 'democratic A.I. exports' argument (see: Figures 5.7 and 5.8). In terms of perhaps the 'most authoritarian' of A.I. exports – smart policing systems – importers have a distinct preference for US-made exports or both US and Chinese offerings, further weakening the argument that China is the only country that exports authoritarian tools or that the US leads 'democratic A.I.' efforts. Further hammering in this point, a greater number of countries import surveillance-purpose A.I. tools from the US compared to China. In terms of exporting A.I. as a repressive tool, China and the US appear comparably involved.

Indeed, further delving into Hypothesis-1, we observe a weak relationship between freedom scores and whether countries prefer Chinese- or American-origin A.I. tools. Countries with higher freedom scores very slightly tend to import US-made A.I. tools, but China is a strong second, nullifying a great degree of regime type effects on A.I. imports. More interestingly, as regime scores improve, countries tend not to buy either from the US or China (suggesting they buy either from the EU or Japan) or from both the US and China. We further observe that electoral autocracies have a tendency to buy more from China, but this is similarly valid for electoral democracies as well as liberal democracies (see: Figures 5.9, 5.10 and Table 5.1). As far as regional variances go, Chinese A.I. exports dominate Africa and Asian continents, while they remain popular in Europe and Latin America as well. It is important to underline that there are no European countries, in our dataset, that are solely buying A.I. infrastructure from the US in our datasets, but five European countries buy solely from China (see Figure 5.13).

The best explanation of A.I. import choices remain GDP per capita and income (see: Figure 5.11 and Table 5.1). Countries with low, lower-middle, and upper-middle income buy dominantly from China, while in high-income countries this gap narrows. Even then, richer

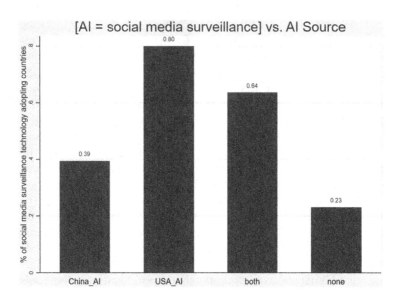

Figure 5.7 Chinese versus US A.I. import preference in sample countries by surveillance-related A.I. tools.

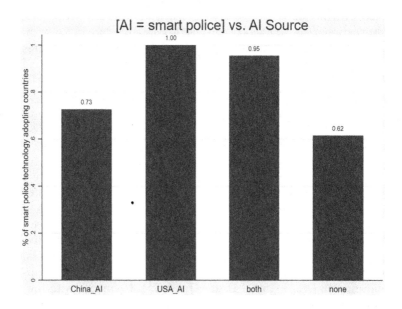

Figure 5.8 Chinese versus US A.I. import preference in sample countries by smart policing-related A.I.

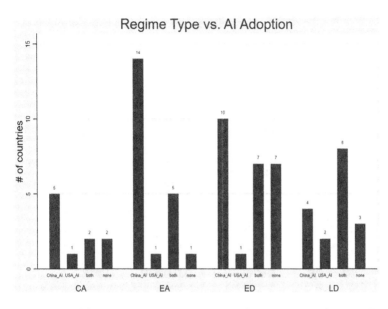

Figure 5.9 Chinese versus US A.I. export preference in sample countries by regime type.

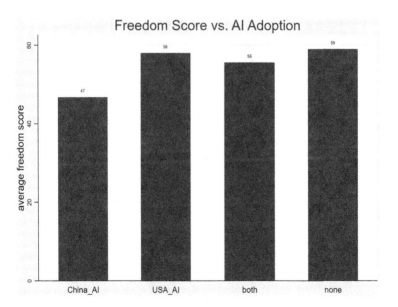

Figure 5.10 Chinese versus US A.I. export preference in sample countries by freedom scores.

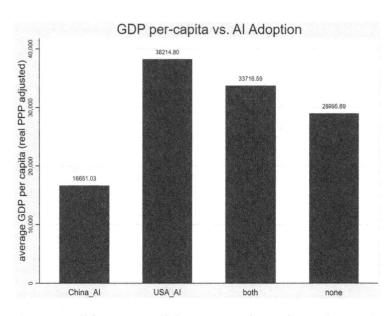

Figure 5.11 Chinese versus US A.I. export preference in sample countries by GDP per capita.

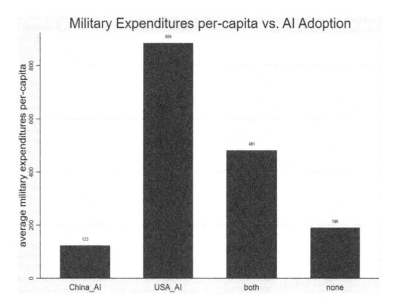

Figure 5.12 Chinese versus US A.I. export preference in sample countries by military spending.

Table 5.1 Multinomial Logit Regression

Eqn	Variables	(1)	(2)	(3)	(4)	(5)	(6)	(7)
		AI source	AI source	AI source	AI source	AI source	AI source	AI source
China_AI	Regime = EA	1.7228 (1.3402)	2.2589 (1.6000)	2.1755 (1.5775)	1.9412 (1.5645)	1.7436 (1.5604)	1.7436 (1.5604)	1.0466 (1.8036)
	Regime = ED	-0.5596 (0.9777)	-0.0121 (1.1033)	0.0829 (1.0915)	-0.0572 (1.1308)	0.1264 (1.0801)	0.1264 (1.0801)	0.6703 (1.4308)
	Regime = LD	-0.6286 (1.1407)	0.4927 (1.4767)	1.2213 (1.5065)	1.3516 (1.6161)	1.2765 (1.5970)	1.2765 (1.5970)	1.7412 (1.6773)
	LNgdppc_2019					-0.4777 (0.8051)	-0.4777 (0.8051)	-0.9035 (1.0229)
	LNgdp_2019					0.4279 (0.5459)	0.4279 (0.5459)	0.7619 (0.5280)
	CHN/US imp. rat.							-0.0122 (0.0446)
	CHN/US imp. gr.							2.7650* (1.5816)
	EUR imp. Growth							-3.4151* (1.7561)
USA_AI	Regime = EA	0.6931 (1.8838)	1.3961 (2.0514)	1.3518 (2.0376)	1.3471 (2.0439)	5.2275 (3.5103)	5.2275 (3.5103)	28.8147*** (3.2972)
	Regime = ED	-1.2528 (1.6369)	-0.6505 (2.1023)	-0.6495 (2.1801)	-0.7278 (2.2883)	3.4148 (3.8786)	3.4148 (3.8786)	-124.8285*** (4.2193)
	Regime = LD	0.2877 (1.5381)	1.9964 (1.7753)	2.1330 (1.8358)	2.1493 (1.8961)	4.6416 (3.5507)	4.6416 (3.5507)	-4.4278 (3.1447)
	LNgdppc_2019					2.2580* (1.3289)	2.2580* (1.3289)	104.3610*** (3.6983)

(Continued)

Eqn	Variables	(1)	(2)	(3)	(4)	(5)	(6)	(7)
		AI source	AI source	AI source	AI source	AI source	AI source	AI source
	LNgdp_2019					0.8505	0.8505	-4.5430***
						(1.1788)	(1.1788)	(0.7579)
	CHN/US imp. rat.							-40.0337***
								(1.6062)
	CHN/US imp. gr.							-438.0349***
								(10.2797)
	EUR imp. growth							302.0774***
								(7.5560)
Both	Regime = EA	1.6094	1.9530	1.9871	1.2224	2.5591	2.5591	4.0372
		(1.4935)	(1.7387)	(1.7161)	(1.7664)	(1.6592)	(1.6592)	(2.5536)
	Regime = ED	-0.0000	0.1111	-0.0686	-0.7744	0.1516	0.1516	-0.0096
		(1.1417)	(1.2616)	(1.2614)	(1.4057)	(1.4816)	(1.4816)	(1.7183)
	Regime = LD	0.9808	1.6360	1.2047	1.5110	1.7403	1.7403	2.7003
		(1.2160)	(1.5768)	(1.7878)	(1.9485)	(1.9483)	(1.9483)	(2.2363)
	LNgdppc_2019					1.4890	1.4890	1.4455
						(0.9747)	(0.9747)	(1.1832)
	LNgdp_2019					0.2503	0.2503	0.3407
						(0.4185)	(0.4185)	(0.6122)
	CHN/US imp. rat.							-0.2831
								(0.1902)
	CHN/US imp. gr.							0.4983
								(1.8645)
	EUR imp. growth							2.5039
								(3.5205)
	Observations	73	73	73	73	72	72	72
	Pseudo R2	0.0653	0.123	0.174	0.228	0.322	0.322	0.545

Robust standard errors in parentheses (*** p<0.01, ** p<0.05, * p<0.1).
Included Controls: region, population, BRI.

countries tend to buy from both China and the US rather than being dependent on either. But most acutely, countries with a higher GDP per capita tend to buy more from the US than China, whereas countries that have a higher GDP tend to buy from both countries. Perhaps as a final nail in the coffin of the 'regime type' argument, countries that have a higher military expenditure budget tend to buy A.I. exports from the US in a larger volume. Countries with lower military budgets clearly prefer Chinese A.I. exports (see: Figure 5.12).

Discussion

Overall, these results increase our skepticism towards the explanatory value of the 'regime type' argument and show a weak relationship between whether a country is democratic or authoritarian and whether it acquires A.I. technology predominantly from China or the US. Rather, current evidence demonstrates that not only authoritarian regimes, but also electoral and liberal democracies tend to import A.I. tools from China, often more exclusively than they import from the US. With the exception of a few wealthy liberal democracies, most countries – liberal democracies, electoral democracies, electoral autocracies, and closed autocracies – all choose Chinese exports, and in most cases, countries with a richer ecosystem of A.I. firms tend to import *both* from China and the US. With these findings, we argue that regime type is not a strong determinant of A.I. acquisition trends, especially in light of the fact that more countries buy smart policing and surveillance tools from the US than they do from China.

Two of the most powerful variables that explain whether countries adopt A.I. through China or the US are military spending, GDP per capita and GDP. Wealthier countries with larger defense budgets tend to prefer US-origin A.I. equipment while China capitalizes on a larger A.I. market that includes all regime types except the wealthiest liberal democracies. In addition, there is currently no strong evidence to support the claim that countries import 'authoritarian A.I. tools' only from China and 'democratic tools' only from the US. Most acutely, countries buy both authoritarian and otherwise A.I. technologies from both China and the US, and in the case of surveillance-oriented technologies, the US has a distinct market edge. Furthermore, current data shows that global competition for A.I. dominance is largely driven by global inequalities – between a smaller group of wealthier countries that can afford to prioritize A.I. ethics and norms and a larger group of developing countries that are seeking more affordable and faster options to integrate emerging technologies into their national strategies.

These findings mean that the scholarship should move beyond the regime type dyad in assessing why countries buy Chinese or American A.I. exports and instead focus on comparative developmental explanations such as growth, regional trade competition, and affordability of technological adoption. Overall, our findings indicate that China will continue to exclusively trade with a larger number of countries, if it is the only country that is able to provide affordable A.I. exports at scale. It is important to underline that this doesn't mean that China is 'better' or 'stronger' in A.I. compared to the US,[3] but merely that its A.I. export model will likely help it stay ahead of the US in terms of the number of countries it trades with exclusively (with no US competition). While important from a policy perspective, Western 'A.I. ethics' discourse will likely remain insignificant in the face of immediate growth and technological advancement needs of developing countries. Given the popularity of Chinese A.I. exports, the majority of countries outside the US/EU alliance ecosystem will find it easy to turn away from Western A.I. exports that are more expensive than developing countries can reliably use, and come with ideological strings attached. Such turn towards Chinese A.I. exports are even visible in the EU-related figures in our datasets, where no country exclusively trades with the US on A.I. issues and opt for both Chinese and American offerings.

To conclude, although US-origin A.I. exports may be technologically more advanced, Chinese export strategy of offering more moderately priced, moderate-capability A.I. tools has resulted in significant popularity of the latter globally. Unless either the US or EU can produce a more imaginative economic technology-transfer model that can render high-tech development more affordable for developing countries, Western A.I. exports will likely remain within the 'rich countries club' and will not be adopted by the rest of the world. If that continues to be the case, China may well lead in A.I. in terms of the number of its trade partners, which can ultimately lead to Chinese diplomatic and political gains in other technology-related issues. In terms of how to alter this momentum, our suggestion is an outlier against other mainstream suggestions that urge building better norms, more comprehensive ethical guidelines, establish stronger Western institutions to safeguard A.I. ethics, or issue targeted sanctions against Chinese A.I. exports or countries that import such tools. While these are important, none of those suggestions are likely to shift developing countries away from Chinese A.I. exports – rather, they will more likely exclude and antagonize these countries, expediting China's ability to form a unified international bloc of developing countries on A.I. technology partnership.

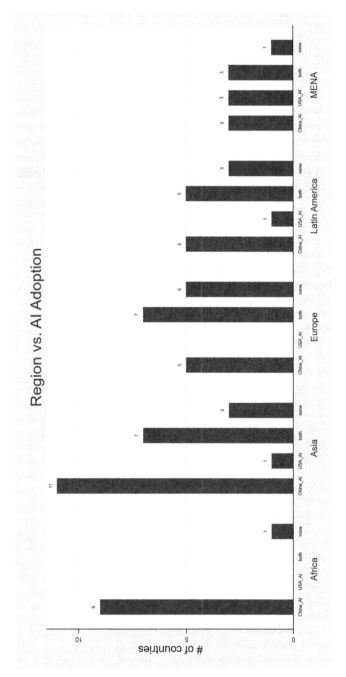

Figure 5.13 Number of countries importing AI from US, China or both by region

Instead, we believe that the US and the EU have to build a new export model that can compete with China at the medium-cost, medium-capability A.I. exports range. Since Western exports are already unaffordable for the majority of the countries advancing in A.I., the only way to link those countries to the Western technology ecosystem is to offer more reliable and better-performing, mid-range exports at scale. We do not suggest either the US or Europe turn away from A.I. ethics or norms, but in order to be able to insist on those priorities, Western exports need to be decisively more preferable over Chinese exports at price-performance ratio. Ultimately, by breaking Western A.I. exports from its small 'rich countries club' bubble and by offering more efficient A.I. technologies can the West produce sufficient leverage to build international partnerships based on truly representative and inclusive global institutions and norms.

Notes

1 https://aiindex.stanford.edu/
2 https://wits.worldbank.org/
3 For a comprehensive study on this, see Castro et al., 2019.

Bibliography

Acemoglu, D., & Robinson, J. A. (2000). Political Losers as a Barrier to Economic Development. *The American Economic Review, 90*(2), 126–130.

Alsheibani, S., Cheung, Y., & Messom, C. (2018). Artificial Intelligence Adoption: AI-readiness at Firm-Level. *PACIS 2018 Proceedings*, 9.

Aly, H. (2020). Digital Transformation, Development and Productivity in Developing Countries: Is Artificial Intelligence a Curse or a Blessing? *Review of Economics and Political Science, ahead-of-print* (ahead-of-print). https://doi.org/10.1108/REPS-11-2019-0145

Campbell, H. (2008). China in Africa: Challenging US global hegemony. *Third World Quarterly, 29*(1), 89–105. https://doi.org/10.1080/01436590701726517

Castro, D., McLaughlin, M., & Chivot, E. (2019). *Who Is Winning the AI Race: China, the EU or the United States?* (p. 106). Center for Data Innovation. https://www2.datainnovation.org/2019-china-eu-us-ai.pdf

Choi, C., & Jee, S. H. (2021). Differential Effects of Information and Communication Technology on (De-) Democratization of Authoritarian Regimes. *International Studies Quarterly, sqab053*. https://doi.org/10.1093/isq/sqab053

Corrales, J., & Westhoff, F. (2006). Information Technology Adoption and Political Regimes. *International Studies Quarterly, 50*(4), 911–933. https://doi.org/10.1111/j.1468-2478.2006.00431.x

Diamond, L. (2010). Liberation Technology. *Journal of Democracy, 21*(3), 69–83. https://doi.org/10.1353/jod.0.0190

Druzin, B., & Gordon, G. S. (2018). Authoritarianism and the Internet. *Law & Social Inquiry, 43*(4), 1427–1457. https://doi.org/10.1111/lsi.12301

Evans, P. B. (1995). *Embedded Autonomy: States and Industrial Transformation*. Princeton University Press. https://press.princeton.edu/books/paperback/9780691037363/embedded-autonomy

Fatima, S., Desouza, K. C., & Dawson, G. S. (2020). National Strategic Artificial Intelligence Plans: A Multi-dimensional Analysis. *Economic Analysis and Policy, 67*, 178–194. https://doi.org/10.1016/j.eap.2020.07.008

Feldstein, S. (2019a). The Road to Digital Unfreedom: How Artificial Intelligence Is Reshaping Repression. *Journal of Democracy, 30*(1), 40–52. https://doi.org/10.1353/jod.2019.0003

Feldstein, S. (2019b, September 17). The Global Expansion of AI Surveillance. *Carnegie Endowment for International Peace.* https://carnegieendowment.org/2019/09/17/global-expansion-of-ai-surveillance-pub-79847

Frank, M. R., Autor, D., Bessen, J. E., Brynjolfsson, E., Cebrian, M., Deming, D. J., Feldman, M., Groh, M., Lobo, J., Moro, E., Wang, D., Youn, H., & Rahwan, I. (2019). Toward Understanding the Impact of Artificial Intelligence on Labor. *Proceedings of the National Academy of Sciences, 116*(14), 6531–6539. https://doi.org/10.1073/pnas.1900949116

Franke, U. (2021). *Artificial Intelligence Diplomacy: Artificial Intelligence Governance as a New External Policy Tool* (PE 662.926; p. 55). European Parliament Directorate-General for Internal Policies. https://www.europarl.europa.eu/RegData/etudes/STUD/2021/662926/IPOL_STU(2021)662926_EN.pdf

Garcia, D. (2021). Stop the Emerging AI Cold War. *Nature, 593*(7858), 169–169. https://doi.org/10.1038/d41586-021-01244-z

Gravett, W. H. (2020). Digital Coloniser? China and Artificial Intelligence in Africa. *Survival, 62*(6), 153–178. https://doi.org/10.1080/00396338.2020.1851098

Greitens, S. C. (2020). *Dealing with Demand for China's Global Surveillance Exports.* Brookings Institution. https://www.brookings.edu/research/dealing-with-demand-for-chinas-global-surveillance-exports/

Haner, J., & Garcia, D. (2019). The Artificial Intelligence Arms Race: Trends and World Leaders in Autonomous Weapons Development. *Global Policy, 10*(3), 331–337. https://doi.org/10.1111/1758-5899.12713

Hausman, J., & McFadden, D. (1984). Specification Tests for the Multinomial Logit Model. *Econometrica, 52*(5), 1219–1240. https://doi.org/10.2307/1910997

Helm, J. M., Swiergosz, A. M., Haeberle, H. S., Karnuta, J. M., Schaffer, J. L., Krebs, V. E., Spitzer, A. I., & Ramkumar, P. N. (2020). Machine Learning and Artificial Intelligence: Definitions, Applications, and Future Directions. *Current Reviews in Musculoskeletal Medicine, 13*(1), 69–76. https://doi.org/10.1007/s12178-020-09600-8

Horowitz, M. C. (2018). Artificial Intelligence, International Competition, and the Balance of Power. *Texas National Security Review, 1*(3). https://tnsr.org/2018/05/artificial-intelligence-international-competition-and-the-balance-of-power/

Horowitz, M. C., Allen, G. C., Kania, E. B., & Scharre, P. (2018). *Strategic Competition in an Era of Artificial Intelligence* (p. 27). Center for a New

American Security. https://www.cnas.org/publications/reports/strategic-competition-in-an-era-of-artificial-intelligence

Johnson, J. (2019). Artificial Intelligence & Future Warfare: Implications for International Security. *Defense & Security Analysis, 35*(2), 147–169. https://doi.org/10.1080/14751798.2019.1600800

Kania, E. B. (2021). Artificial Intelligence in China's Revolution in Military Affairs. *Journal of Strategic Studies, 44*(4), 515–542. https://doi.org/10.1080/01402390.2021.1894136

Kimber, R. (1991). Artificial Intelligence and the Study of Democracy. *Social Science Computer Review, 9*(3), 381–398. https://doi.org/10.1177/089443939100900303

Kliman, D., & Grace, A. (2018). *Power Play: Addressing China's Belt and Road Strategy* (p. 44). Center for a New American Security. https://www.cnas.org/publications/reports/power-play

Lamensch, M. (2021, July 9). Authoritarianism Has Been Reinvented for the Digital Age. *Centre for International Governance Innovation*. https://www.cigionline.org/articles/authoritarianism-has-been-reinvented-for-the-digital-age/

Leslie, D., Burr, C., Aitken, M., Cowls, J., Katell, M., & Briggs, M. (2021). *Artificial Intelligence, Human Rights, Democracy, and the Rule of Law: A Primer* (SSRN Scholarly Paper ID 3817999). Social Science Research Network. https://doi.org/10.2139/ssrn.3817999

Levy, F. (2018). Computers and Populism: Artificial Intelligence, Jobs, and Politics in the Near Term. *Oxford Review of Economic Policy, 34*(3), 393–417. https://doi.org/10.1093/oxrep/gry004

Malmborg, F. af, & Trondal, J. (2021). Discursive Framing and Organizational Venues: Mechanisms of Artificial Intelligence Policy Adoption. *International Review of Administrative Sciences*. https://doi.org/10.1177/00208523211007533

Meltzer, J. P., & Kerry, C. F. (2021, February 17). Strengthening International Cooperation on Artificial Intelligence. *Brookings Institution*.https://www.brookings.edu/research/strengthening-international-cooperation-on-artificial-intelligence/

Milner, H. V. (2006). The Digital Divide: The Role of Political Institutions in Technology Diffusion. *Comparative Political Studies, 39*(2), 176–199. https://doi.org/10.1177/0010414005282983

Nemitz, P. (2018). Constitutional Democracy and Technology in the Age of Artificial Intelligence. *Philosophical Transactions of the Royal Society A: Mathematical, Physical and Engineering Sciences, 376*(2133), 20180089. https://doi.org/10.1098/rsta.2018.0089

Petralia, S. (2021). GPTs and Growth: Evidence on the Technological Adoption of Electrical and Electronic Technologies in the 1920s. *European Review of Economic History, 25*(3), 571–608. https://doi.org/10.1093/erehj/heaa022

Polyakova, A., & Meserole, C. (2019). *Exporting Digital Authoritarianism* (p. 22). Brookings Institution. https://www.brookings.edu/research/exporting-digital-authoritarianism/

Roberts, H., Cowls, J., Morley, J., Taddeo, M., Wang, V., & Floridi, L. (2021). The Chinese Approach to Artificial Intelligence: An Analysis of Policy, Ethics, and Regulation. *AI & SOCIETY, 36*(1), 59–77. https://doi.org/10.1007/s00146-020-00992-2

Rød, E. G., & Weidmann, N. B. (2015). Empowering Activists or Autocrats? The Internet in Authoritarian Regimes. *Journal of Peace Research, 52*(3), 338–351. https://doi.org/10.1177/0022343314555782

Schiff, D. S., Schiff, K. J., & Pierson, P. (2021). Assessing Public Value Failure in Government Adoption of Artificial Intelligence. *Public Administration.* https://doi.org/10.1111/padm.12742

Small, K. A., & Hsiao, C. (1985). Multinomial Logit Specification Tests. *International Economic Review, 26*(3), 619–627. https://doi.org/10.2307/2526707

Stier, S. (2015). Political Determinants of E-government Performance Revisited: Comparing Democracies and Autocracies. *Government Information Quarterly, 32*(3), 270–278.

Unver, A. (2018). *Artificial Intelligence, Authoritarianism and the Future of Political Systems* (SSRN Scholarly Paper ID 3331635). Social Science Research Network. https://papers.ssrn.com/abstract=3331635

Viscusi, G., Collins, A., & Florin, M.-V. (2020). Governments' Strategic Stance toward Artificial Intelligence: An Interpretive Display on Europe. *Proceedings of the 13th International Conference on Theory and Practice of Electronic Governance*, 44–53. https://doi.org/10.1145/3428502.3428508

Wang, P. (2019). On Defining Artificial Intelligence. *Journal of Artificial General Intelligence, 10*(2), 1–37. https://doi.org/10.2478/jagi-2019-0002

Weber, F. D., & Schütte, R. (2019). State-of-the-art and Adoption of Artificial Intelligence in Retailing. *Digital Policy, Regulation and Governance, 21*(3), 264–279. https://doi.org/10.1108/DPRG-09-2018-0050

Webster, C., & Ivanov, S. (2020). Robotics, Artificial Intelligence, and the Evolving Nature of Work. In B. George & J. Paul (Eds.), *Digital Transformation in Business and Society: Theory and Cases* (pp. 127–143). Springer International Publishing. https://doi.org/10.1007/978-3-030-08277-2_8

Wright, N. D. (2020). *Artificial Intelligence and Democratic Norms* (Sharp Power and Democratic Resilience, p. 20). National Endowment for Democracy. https://www.ned.org/wp-content/uploads/2020/07/Artificial-Intelligence-Democratic-Norms-Meeting-Authoritarian-Challenge-Wright.pdf

Zeng, J. (2020). Artificial Intelligence and China's Authoritarian Governance. *International Affairs, 96*(6), 1441–1459. https://doi.org/10.1093/ia/iiaa172

Zerfass, A., Hagelstein, J., & Tench, R. (2020). Artificial Intelligence in Communication Management: A Cross-national Study on Adoption and Knowledge, Impact, Challenges and Risks. *Journal of Communication Management, 24*(4), 377–389. https://doi.org/10.1108/JCOM-10-2019-0137

Index

Note: **Bold** page numbers refer to tables; *Italic* page numbers refer to figures and page number followed by "n" refer to end notes.

Printed in the United States
by Baker & Taylor Publisher Services